Study Guide

America's Courts and the Criminal Justice System

NINTH EDITION

David W. Neubauer
University of New Orleans

Prepared by

Clayton Steenberg
Arkansas State University Mountain Home

THOMSON
WADSWORTH

Australia • Brazil • Canada • Mexico • Singapore • Spain • United Kingdom • United States

ISBN-10: 0-495-38274-4
ISBN-13: 978-0-495-38274-4

Thomson Higher Education
10 Davis Drive
Belmont, CA 94002-3098
USA

For more information about our products, contact us at:
Thomson Learning Academic Resource Center
1-800-423-0563

For permission to use material from this text or product, submit a request online at
http://www.thomsonrights.com.
Any additional questions about permissions can be submitted by email to **thomsonrights@thomson.com.**

Table of Contents

Chapter 1
COURTS, CRIME AND CONTROVERSY

LEARNING OBJECTIVES

After reading this chapter, students should understand

- the three major components of the American criminal justice system.
- the fragmented nature of the American criminal justice system, including the significance of the dual court system.
- the ways in which American criminal justice can be considered both a system and a nonsystem.
- the identity and nature of the various courthouse actors, including prosecutors, attorneys, judges, defendants, and victims.
- the steps of the formal criminal justice process, from criminal act to sentencing and appeal.
- the major sources of law in the U.S., including constitutional, statute, and case law.
- the role of discretion in the day-to-day application of the law.
- the crime control and due process models of justice elaborated by Herbert Packer.

CHAPTER OUTLINE

I. **The Courts and the Criminal Justice System**
   A. Three Main Components of Criminal Justice System
      1. Police
      2. Courts
      3. Corrections
   B. An Interdependent Criminal Justice System
   C. Fragmented Criminal Justice Nonsystem
   D. Tensions and Conflicts

II. **Finding the Courthouse**
   1. 17,000 courthouses
   2. Dual Court System (state and federal)
   3. Trial and Appellate Courts

III. **Identifying the Actors in the Courthouse**
   A. Prosecutors
      1. Independent and fragmented
      2. Most powerful of major actors
   B. Defense Attorneys
      1. Most defendants indigent and attorneys are paid for by government
      2. Few defendants hire their own private attorney
   C. Judges
      1. Most state judges elected
      2. Federal judges nominated by President and approved by Senate

1

D. Defendants and Their Victims
1. Defendants and victims disproportionately poor, uneducated, and minority males
2. Victims are seen as more important in the courts than before

IV. Following the Steps of the Process
A. Crime
B. Arrest
C. Initial Appearance
D. Bail
E. Preliminary hearing
F. Charging decision
G. Grand jury
H. Arraignment
I. Evidence
J. Plea negotiation
K. Trial
L. Sentencing
M. Appeal

V. Law on the Books
1. Legal and structural components of the judiciary
2. Sources of laws
    a. Constitutions (state and federal)
    b. U.S. Constitution is supreme
    c. U.S. Supreme Court decisions
3. Statutes by legislative bodies
4. Administrative regulations
5. Cases decided by the courts

VI. Law in Action
1. Focuses on the application of law
2. Stresses the importance of discretion

VII. Courts and Controversy
1. Crime control model
    a. Conservative model
    b. Suppression of crime is a priority
2. Due process model
    a. Liberal model
    b. Rights and freedoms of individuals are the most important

VIII. Conclusion
1. Public expects the making of law will solve all crime problems.
2. Television and other media sources lead to distorted information about criminal justice and the courts.

KEY TERMS

crime control mode l- A perspective on the criminal justice process based on the proposition that the most important function of criminal justice is the repression of crime, focusing on efficiency as a principal measure. (17)

criminal justice system - Agencies and institutions directly involved in the implementation of public policy concerning crime, mainly the law enforcement agencies, courts, and corrections. (6)

due process model - A philosophy of criminal justice based on the assumption that an individual is innocent until proven guilty and has a right to protection from arbitrary power of the state. (19)

CHAPTER SUMMARY

Each year governments spend almost 185 billion dollars on civil and criminal justice. Approximately 2.4 million people work in the criminal justice system. Police make around 13.5 million arrests every year, and there are 7 million people under some form of correctional supervision. The criminal justice system is a massive enterprise.

The criminal justice system has three major components: police, courts and corrections. The relationships between and within these components are not smooth and efficient. There are thousands of police, court, and corrections agencies in this country. Cases flow through these components and what happens in each component affects the other components. Thus we speak of a criminal justice system. However, there is no centralized control or coordination of all these agencies. There is tension and conflict between agencies. In this sense it is a nonsystem.

There are roughly 17,000 courthouses in the U.S. We have a dual court system—we have both state and federal courts. Trial courts hear evidence and return verdicts. Appellate courts correct any errors made by trial courts. The primary actors in courts are prosecutors, defense attorneys, judges, defendants, and victims.

The processing of a criminal case (criminal procedure) and the terminology vary somewhat from jurisdiction to jurisdiction, and felony cases involve more steps than misdemeanor cases. The description below is one of a typical felony case in a typical jurisdiction.

After arrest, arrestees will be brought before a judge for an initial appearance. Arrestees will be advised of the charges and their rights and bail will be set. Arrestees who cannot post or make bail will be detained in the jail pending trial.

If the case is a felony, there will be a preliminary hearing. The judge must determine whether there is probable cause to take the case to the grand jury. A prosecutor will then review the case and decide upon the charges. The prosecutor will then take the case to the grand jury and ask them to indict the defendant. If indicted, the defendant will be arraigned on the charges. At arraignment, the defendant will be advised of his or her rights, and also of the charges, and he or she will be asked to enter a plea.

Prior to trial, each side has an opportunity to find out something about the other side's evidence. This process is called discovery. After discovery, the parties may attempt to avoid trial by engaging in plea bargaining or negotiating.

If the defendant does not plead guilty, the case will be set for trial in the appropriate trial court. Trial may be with or without a jury (bench trial). After presentation of the evidence, arguments of attorneys and instructions by the judges, the jury will generally return a verdict.

If the verdict is guilty, the defendant will be sentenced. After sentencing, the defendant may appeal the verdict to a higher or appellate court. The conviction may also be challenged indirectly or collaterally through *habeas corpus* or another form of collateral attack.

The criminal justice system operates under legal rules. The rules are written and found in many sources. The U.S. Constitution is the supreme law of the land, and is the most important source of law. The U.S. Supreme Court has the final say on the meaning of the Constitution and its opinions are extremely important. Statutory law, which is passed by the legislature, is another important source of law. However, the system does not always operate according to the law (law on the books). To understand how the system works, we must look at the law in action (how the system really works).

We expect courts to solve most of society's controversies and problems. We rely heavily on the criminal justice system to maintain order. There are two basic models of the criminal justice process. The crime control model is a conservative model and stresses repression of crime and quick efficient processing. The due process model is a liberal model and stresses the rights and freedoms of individuals.

PRACTICE TEST BANK

Multiple Choice

1. Each year state, federal and local governments spend around $_____ billion on civil and criminal justice.
    a.   100
    b.   185
    c.   200
    d.   250

2. The American criminal justice system (and its components) are both _____.
    a.   centrally controlled and internally isolated
    b.   unitary and fragmented
    c.   interdependent and fragmented
    d.   fragmented and centrally controlled

3. The three main components of the American criminal justice system are _____.
    a.   prosecutors, judges, and defense attorneys
    b.   police, law enforcement, and courts
    c.   police, courts, and probation
    d.   police, courts, and corrections

4. In the U.S. there are over _____ different state, federal, and local law enforcement agencies.
    a.   1,000
    b.   17,000
    c.   55,000
    d.   100,000

5. The relationships between the components and agencies in the American criminal justice system are _____.
    a.   all coordinated by the federal government
    b.   controlled by the U.S. Supreme Court
    c.   managed by state and federal prosecutors
    d.   characterized by tension and conflict

6. The term dual court system refers to the fact that in America we have _____.
    a.   civil and criminal courts
    b.   law and equity jurisdiction
    c.   state (incl. local) and federal courts
    d.   national and international tribunals

7. Most courts in this country are _____ courts.
    a. trial
    b. federal
    c. appellate
    d. chancery

8. The most influential courthouse actor is the _____.
    a. defense attorney
    b. judge
    c. clerk of courts
    d. prosecutor

9. Most state court judges are _____.
    a. elected
    b. appointed by the governor
    c. appointed by the legislature
    d. appointed by the state Supreme Court

10. Police make slightly more than _____ million arrests for nontraffic offenses each year.
    a. 10
    b. 13
    c. 20
    d. 35

11. After a person is arrested and booked, the next step will usually be _____.
    a. initial appearance
    b. preliminary hearing
    c. arraignment
    d. charging decision

12. At the preliminary hearing, the prosecutor must show _____ cause to believe the defendant was involved in a crime.
    a. rational
    b. objective
    c. subjective
    d. probable

13. Grand jury review is required in _____.
    a. all state felony cases
    b. all federal felony cases
    c. all state and federal felony cases
    d. all federal misdemeanor cases

14. A trial before a judge without a jury is called a _____ trial.
    a. bar
    b. bench
    c. equity
    d. preliminary

15. The dominant reality of contemporary corrections is _____.
    a. indeterminate sentences
    b. probation for violent felons
    c. prison overcrowding
    d. electronic monitoring and house arrest for convicted felons

16. The most important goal for the crime control model is _____.
    a. repression of crime
    b. reducing prison populations
    c. preventing conviction of the innocent
    d. respecting the rights of defendants

17. The due process model emphasizes _____.
    a. protection of society
    b. protecting the rights of individuals
    c. quick and speedy processing of cases
    d. reducing prison populations

18. The due process model is generally associated with _____ politics.
    a. reactionary
    b. conservative
    c. socialist
    d. liberal

19. Politicians and voters today tend to _____.
    a. have an accurate understanding of how the criminal justice system works
    b. do not let politics influence their views and decisions
    c. support decriminalization of laws against cocaine and heroin
    d. see passing new laws as the solution to most problems

20. Media presentations on crime and justice are usually _____.
    a. based on empirical research
    b. accurate reflections of the real world in general
    c. inaccurate and distorted
    d. unbiased

True-False

1. Our criminal justice system and its components are interdependent, fragmented, and suffer tension and conflict.
    a. true
    b. false

2. The defense attorney is the most influential and powerful figure in the courts.
    a. true
    b. false

3. The three major components of the criminal justice system are police, courts and corrections.
    a. true
    b. false

4. America has a dual court system.
    a. true
    b. false.

5. The American criminal justice system and its components are decentralized.
    a. true
    b. false

6. There are roughly 100,000 courthouses in the U.S. today.
    a. true
    b. false

7. Major trial courts conduct the initial proceedings in a felony case.
    a. true
    b. false

8. Appellate courts review decisions made by trial courts and lower appellate courts.
    a. true
    b. false

9. The U.S. Supreme Court hears, decides and writes opinions on around 200 cases each year.
    a. true
    b. false

10. The organization of prosecutors in the U.S. is not fragmented.
    a. true
    b. false

11. Most criminal defendants hire their own private lawyer.
    a.   true
    b.   false

12. The initial appearance will usually be the first time an arrested person will see a judge.
    a.   true
    b   false

13. Federal judges are elected.
    a.   true
    b.   false

14. In the due process model, the system can be viewed as an obstacle course to conviction.
    a.   true
    b.   false

15. The rights of individuals are the first priority in the crime control model.
    a.   true
    b.   false

Fill in the Blank

1. The most influential of the courthouse actors is the _____.

2. A trial by a judge without a jury is called a _____ trial.

3. Because America has both state and federal courts it is said to have a _____ court system.

4. The process by which each side in a lawsuit reveals at least some of its evidence to the other side is called _____.

5. If the grand jury refuses to indict, it returns a no bill or no _____ bill.

6. One of the most significant pretrial motions filed by defendants is a motion to suppress _____.

7. The crime control and due process models were first developed by Herbert _____.

8. The court that has the greatest impact on criminal justice nationwide is the U.S. _____ Court.

9. In felony cases, the defendant is required to enter a plea at a formal proceeding called _____.

10. There are approximately _____ million persons in America in prison or on probation or parole.

11. As compared to misdemeanors, the processing of _____ cases is more complex.

12. During plea _____ the defense and prosecution will attempt to reach a plea bargain and avoid trial.

13. The three main components of the criminal justice system are police, courts and _____.

14. Roughly _____ million Americans earn their living by working in the criminal justice system.

15. One of the most important things that occur at the initial appearance is the setting of _____ which may allow the defendant to be released.

Essay

1. Describe the steps in a typical felony case from arrest to appeal. Briefly describe what happens at each stage.

2. What does the author of the text mean when he says that criminal justice can be viewed as both a system and a nonsystem? Be sure to provide examples.

3. Why are decisions of the U.S. Supreme Court on constitutional issues in criminal justice so important? Briefly discuss one important decision.

4. Discuss, describe, compare and contrast trial courts and appellate courts. Be sure to provide examples.

5. Describe the major steps in a criminal trial. Explain what happens at each step.

CHAPTER 1 ANSWER KEY

Multiple Choice

1—b	2—c	3—d	4—b	5—d
6—c	7—a	8—d	9—a	10—b
11—a	12—d	13—b	14—b	15—c
16—a	17—b	18—d	19—d	20—c

True-False

1—T	2—F	3—T	4—T	5—T
6—F	7—F	8—T	9—F	10—F
11—F	12—T	13—F	14—T	15—F

Fill in the Blank

1—prosecutor	2—bench	3—dual	4—discovery
5—true	6—evidence	7—Packer	8—Supreme
9—arraignment	10—7	11—felony	12—negotiation
13—corrections	14—2.4	15—bail	

Chapter 2
LAW AND CRIME

LEARNING OBJECTIVES

After reading this chapter, students should understand
- the basis for law.
- the various sources of law.
- the adversarial system of justice.
- the various rights of the criminally accused.
- civil law as a means of settling disputes.
- the various civil remedies.
- the elements of a crime.
- the effects of criminal law on the courts.

CHAPTER OUTLINE

I. **The Basis of law: The Common Law Heritage**
  A. Judge-Made-Law
  B. Precedent
  C. Multiple Sources of Law
    1. Constitutions
    2. Statutes
    3. Administrative Regulations
    4. Judicial Decisions

II. **The Adversary System**
  A. Safeguards
  B. Presumption of Innocence and Burden of Proof on Government

III. **Rights of the Accused**
  A. Due Process
  B. Bill of Rights

IV. **Civil Law**
  A. Basis for Filing a Civil Suit
  B. Remedies
    1. Monetary judgment
    2. Declaratory judgment
    3. Injunction
  C. Using Civil Remedies to Fight Crime
  D. Civil liability of Criminal Justice Officials

V. **Criminal Law**
    1. Felonies
    2. Misdemeanors

VI. **Elements of a Crime (*corpus delicti*)**
    A.   Guilty Act (*actus reus*)
    B.   Guilty Intent (*mens rea*)
    C.   Fusion of Guilty Act and Guilty Intent
    D.   Attendant Circumstances
    E.   Results

VII. **Legal Defenses**

VIII. **Effects of the Criminal Law on the Courts**
    A.   Criminal Law and Inconsistencies
    B.   Criminal Law and Plea Bargaining
    C.   Criminal Law and Sentencing

XI. **Conclusion**
    1.   As society changes, crime changes, and the criminal law changes.
    2.   Courts respond and change as law, society and crime change

KEY TERMS

administrative regulations - Rules and regulations adopted by administrative agencies that have the force of law. (29)

adversary system - A proceeding in which the opposing sides have the opportunity to present their evidence and arguments. (30)

Anglo-American law - The American legal system See *common law*. (27)

attempt - An act done with the intent to commit a crime, an overt act toward its commission, the failure to complete the crime, and the apparent possibility of committing it. (41)

attendant (accompanying) circumstances - Conditions surrounding a criminal act—for example, the amount of money stolen in a theft. (42)

beyond a reasonable doubt - Burden of proof required by law to convict a defendant in a criminal case. (31)

Bill of Rights - The first ten amendments to the U.S. Constitution, guaranteeing certain rights and liberties to the people. (33)

civil law - Law governing private parties; other than criminal law. (34)

common law - Law developed in England by judges who made legal decisions in the absence of written law. Such decisions served as precedents and became "common" to all of England. Common law is judge made, it uses precedent, and it is found in multiple sources. (27)

constitution - The fundamental rules that determine how those who govern are selected, the procedures by which they operate, and the limits to their powers. (29)

contract - A legally enforceable agreement between two or more parties. (35)

corpus delicti - The body or substance of a crime, composed of two elements—the act and the criminal agency producing it. (40)

criminal law - Laws passed by government that define and prohibit antisocial behavior. (38)

declaratory judgment - Judicial pronouncement declaring the legal rights of parties involved in an actual case or controversy. (36)

defendant - The person or party against whom a lawsuit or prosecution is brought. (36)

domestic relations - Relating to the home; the law of divorce, custody, support, adoption, and so on. (36)

due process of law - A right guaranteed in the Fifth, Sixth, and Fourteenth Amendments of the U.S. Constitution and generally understood to mean the due course of legal proceedings according to the rules and forms established for the protection of private rights. (31)

elements of a crime - Five principles of a crime that are critical to the statutory definition of crimes: guilty act, guilty intent, relationship between guilty act and guilty intent, attendant circumstances, and results. (40)

felony - The more serious of the two basic types of criminal behavior, usually bearing a possible penalty of one year or more in prison. (39)

fusion of the guilty act and guilty intent - One of the components of a crime. Criminal law requires that the guilty intent and the guilty act occur together. See *elements of a crime*. (42)

guilty act (actus reus) - Requirement that, for an act to be considered criminal, the individual must have committed an overt act that resulted in criminal harm. See *elements of a crime*. (41)
guilty intent (mens rea) - Mental state required for a crime. (42)

incorporation - The theory that the Bill of Rights has been incorporated or absorbed into the due process clause of the Fourteenth Amendment, thereby making it applicable to the states. (34)

inheritance - Property received from a dead person, either by effect of intestacy or through a will. (36)

injunction - A court order directing someone to do something or to refrain from doing something. (37)

in rem - Against a thing; a legal proceeding instituted to obtain decrees or judgments against property. (38)

judge-made law - The common law as developed in form and content by judges or judicial decisions. (27)

judgment - The official decision of a court concerning a legal matter. (36)

juvenile delinquency - An act committed by a juvenile for which an adult could be prosecuted in a criminal court. (44)

law - Body of rules enacted by public officials in a legitimate manner and backed by the force of the state. (26)

legal defense - Legally recognized justification for illegal actions, or acceptance that individuals were not legally responsible for their actions. (42)

misdemeanor - Lesser of the two basic types of crime, usually punishable by no more than one year in jail. (39)

monetary damage - Compensatory damages payment for actual losses suffered by a plaintiff. Punitive damages—money awarded by a court to a person who has been harmed in a malicious or willful way. (36)

municipal ordinance - Law passed by a local unit of government. (29)

plaintiff - The person or party who initiates a lawsuit. (36)

precedent - A case previously decided that serves as a legal guide for the resolution of subsequent cases. (27)

preponderance of the evidence - In civil law, the standard of proof required to prevail at trial. To win, the plaintiff must show that the greater weight, or preponderance, of the evidence supports his or her version of the facts. (31)

presumption of innocence - Assumption that whenever a person is charged with a crime, he or she is innocent until proved guilty. The defendant is presumed to be innocent, and the burden is on the state to prove guilt beyond a reasonable doubt. (31)

procedural law - Law that outlines the legal processes to be followed in starting, conducting, and finishing a lawsuit. (30)

property - Legal right to use or dispose of particular things or subjects. (36)

remedy - Vindication of a claim of right; a legal procedure by which a right is enforced or the violation of a right is prevented or compensated. (36)

result A consequence; an outcome. (42)

stare decisis - Latin phrase meaning "let the decision stand." The doctrine that principles of law established in earlier judicial decisions should be accepted as authoritative in similar subsequent cases. (27)

statute - A written law enacted by a legislature. (29)

substantive law - Law that deals with the content or substance of the law—for example, the legal grounds for divorce. (30)

CHAPTER SUMMARY

Law is born out of the necessity to settle disputes of human conflict. Law is defined as a body of rules enacted by public officials in a legitimate manner and backed by the force of the state. America's legal system has roots in the Anglo-Saxon common law system of England and is known as Anglo-American law. This system first began appearing in England after 1066 as rulers introduced central government and began to establish courts of law. Based on common or general customs, common law is the basis for the legal systems of most English-speaking nations.

Common law has three unique attributes: it was judge-made law, based on precedent, and found in multiple sources (uncodified). Before legislatures began to introduce laws (statutes) in the 20th Century, judges were largely responsible for making the law. The doctrine of precedent or *stare decisis* allowed the courts to promote fairness and consistency, and allowed for gradual changes to problems. It also supports the idea that courts are fair and impartial, and are not imposing their own personal values.

Multiple sources of law are generally divided into four general groups: constitutions, statutes, administrative regulations, and court decisions. Constitutions are the dominant form of law. The U.S. Constitution is the supreme law of the land. It spells out rights and government powers. Statutes are laws enacted by legislatures and municipal ordinances fall into this category, as they are enacted by local government. Administrative regulations are the most numerous, as they are enacted by the many and various governmental bureaucracies and agencies. Judicial decisions in essence make law through interpretation, as the Supreme Court has been called an ongoing constitutional convention. In their opinions, courts interpret or make the common law and interpret the meaning of constitutions, statutes, ordinances and administrative regulations.

Our adversarial form of justice pits prosecutors against defense attorneys in a venue set up to protect the rights of the accused through legal devices. In the adversary systems, each side presents its best case and has an opportunity to challenge the other side's case. The judge is supposed to referee the conflict in court. Further, the judge and jury are supposed to be the neutral decision makers. Many of the rights in the Bill of Rights now apply to the states. They have been incorporated (or applied) to the states through the due process clause of the Fourteenth Amendment.

The two major types of law are criminal law and civil law. Civil suits are used to settle disputes between individuals, groups of individuals or other legal fictions. The civil law deals with private wrongs, while the criminal law deals with public wrongs. Civil remedies may result in monetary judgment, declaratory judgment or an injunction. Preponderance of evidence is the burden of proof required for a victory. In civil courts, it is a much lower standard than the proof beyond a reasonable doubt required in criminal proceedings. The majority of court cases are civil disputes and the government has even started to use civil law as a means to fight crime, such as drug dealing. Parallel criminal and civil proceedings are being used more today than ever before.

Criminal law is used to prosecute and punish harms or violation against the public or state. The purpose of the criminal law is to protect the public. Misdemeanors and felonies are criminal offenses and tried in criminal courts. The substantive criminal law defines offenses, punishments and defenses. The procedural criminal law sets out the steps in the process of enforcing the substantive criminal law. The procedural law includes the procedural rights of defendants such as the right to a jury trial and to confront and cross-examine adverse witnesses.

Crimes are defined in the substantive criminal law. These definitions are referred to as elements of a crime or *corpus delicti*. Elements of a crime are based on five general principles: a guilty act (*actus reus*), a guilty intent or guilty mind *(mens rea)*, that the guilty act and guilty intent be related, attendant circumstances, and specific results. Various degrees of intent requirements add to the puzzle and attempts can also be prosecuted and punished. There are various legal defenses to crime, as criminal acts must be voluntary. Duress and insanity are two common defenses.

Because laws are generally enacted piecemeal, judges and prosecutors are on the front line. The courtroom work group uses plea bargaining as a tool to expedite disposition of cases. As overloaded courts work just to keep up, legislatures continue to enact new crimes and harsher penalties, placing more of a burden on already overtaxed justice system.

The law on the books is abstract, while the law in action, such as jury verdicts and rulings by judges, is more concrete and may or may not coincide with the law on the books. As we do not live in a static world, law is an integral part of society and must be proactive or constantly changing to keep up with a constantly changing society.

PRACTICE TEST BANK

Multiple Choice

1. In what year did common law first appear in England?
    a. 1000 B.C.
    b. 1066 A.D.
    c. 1600 A.D.
    d. 1900 A.D.

2. Violations of civil law may be punished by _____.
    a. a year or more in prison
    b. less than one year in jail
    c. probation
    d. monetary award

3. *Actus reus* refers to _____.
    a. the body of the crime
    b. guilty intent
    c. guilty act
    d. guilty conscience

4. Law that is found in many sources is generally referred to as _____.
    a. codified
    b. uncodified
    c. substantive
    d. statutory

5. A court order directing a specific action or lack of action is known as an _____.
    a. interdict
    b. injunction
    c. indictment
    d. interdiction

6. Laws or statutes passed by local government are known as _____.
    a. administrative regulations
    b. case law
    c. municipal ordinances
    d. common law

7. What is the burden of proof required for a party to prevail in a civil lawsuit?
    a. beyond a reasonable doubt
    b. probable cause
    c. preponderance of evidence
    d. grand jury indictment

8.   America's common law tradition is also referred to as _____.
     a.   Anglican law
     b.   Anglo-American law
     c.   constitutional law
     d.   Judaeo-American law

9.   Legislatures did not become a principal source of law until _____.
     a.   1776
     b.   the 19th Century
     c.   1865
     d.   the 20th Century

10. Criminal acts must be _____.
     a.   malicious
     b.   voluntary
     c.   with depraved heart
     d.   merely perpetrated

11. The doctrine of "let the decision stand" is also known as _____.
     a.   *stare decisis*
     b.   *decisio precede*
     c.   *stare in judicio*
     d.   *in rem*

12. Court opinions expounding the common law or interpreting statutes or constitutions are known as _____.
     a.   procedural law
     b.   substantive law
     c.   statutory law
     d.   case law

13. The most common remedy in civil cases is _____.
     a.   declaratory judgment
     b.   injunction
     c.   monetary damages
     d.   fines

14. The person against whom a lawsuit is brought is the _____.
     a.   appellant
     b.   plaintiff
     c.   victim
     d.   defendant

15. The _____ Amendment to the U.S. Constitution provides a right to counsel.
   a. Fourth
   b. Fifth
   c. Sixth
   d. Eighth

16. A common civil remedy in drug cases is _____.
   a. declaratory judgment
   b. an injunction
   c. asset forfeiture
   d. monetary damages

17. The protections of the Fifth, Sixth, and Fourteenth Amendments during a criminal proceeding are part of a defendant's right to _____.
   a. declaratory judgment
   b. procedural due process
   c. the presumption of evidence
   d. substantive due process rights

18. The U.S. Constitution is a relatively _____.
   a. long document, with over 40,000 words
   b. short-sighted document, with little meaning today
   c. short document of some 4,300 words
   d. complicated document

19. Differences in degrees of seriousness provide prosecutors with a means for _____.
   a. convictions
   b. acquittals
   c. individualized justice
   d. plea bargaining

20. A statute is a law enacted by _____.
   a. legislatures
   b. judges
   c. governors
   d. governmental bureaucracies

True-False

1. A person may not be prosecuted both civilly and criminally for the same act.
    a.   true
    b.   false

2. Unlike all the other states, Louisiana derives its civil code from Napoleonic Code.
    a.   true
    b.   false

3. The two major actors in the adversary system are the prosecutor and the defense attorney.
    a.   true
    b.   false

4. The Fifth and Fourteenth Amendments to the U.S. Constitution mention due process.
    a.   true
    b.   false

5. The law in action is considered as abstract.
    a.   true
    b.   false

6. The Eighth Amendment prohibits unreasonable searches and seizures.
    a.   true
    b.   false

7. Civil suits may only be filed by individual citizens.
    a.   true
    b.   false

8. The amount of money or goods stolen would be an example of an attendant circumstance.
    a.   true
    b.   false

9. Penalties for attempt are generally more severe than the completed act.
    a.   true
    b.   false

10. Under tort law, an injury may only involve physical harm.
    a.   true
    b.   false

11. A statute is a law enacted by judges.
    a.   true
    b.   false

12. Substantive law deals only with the procedural processes of court proceedings.
   a. true
   b. false

13. Because it can be precisely defined, justice is a key element of law.
   a. true
   b. false

14. Parallel criminal and civil proceedings are being used more today than ever before.
   a. true
   b. false

15. Duress is not a defense recognized by law.
   a. true
   b. false

Fill in the Blank

1. Suing a landowner/property manager for liability is commonly referred to as
   _____ liability.

2. The _____ Amendment prohibits unreasonable searches and seizures.

3. The due process clause is applicable to the state through the _____
   Amendment.

4. All _____ of a crime must be proven for an individual to be convicted of that
   crime.

5. Crimes against the public or state are tried under _____ law.

6. The Latin phrase meaning "body of the crime" is _____ *delicti*.

7. _____ law dealt with the content or substance of the law.

8. Offenders convicted of a _____ are generally sentenced to a year or more in prison.

9. The area of civil law that deals with injury is known as _____ law.

10 _____ *reus* is Latin for "guilty act."

11. The first ten Amendments to the U.S. constitution are collectively known as the Bill of
   _____.

12. In the American criminal justice system, defendants have a presumption of _____.

13. An individual who initiates a civil suit is known as the _____.

14. The _____ Court has been termed an ongoing constitutional convention.

15. The U.S. _____ is the supreme law of the land.

Essay

1. List and discuss the elements of a crime. Be sure to provide an example of each.

2. Discuss and explain the importance of the Bill of Rights to American criminal justice. Be sure to provide examples.

3. List and discuss the safeguards of the American adversarial system of justice. Be sure to provide at least one example

4. What are the major sources of law? List, discuss, and give examples.

5. Compare and contrast civil and criminal law and proceedings. Be sure to provide examples of each.

CHAPTER 2 ANSWER KEY

Multiple Choice

1—a	2—d	3—c	4—b	5—b
6—c	7—c	8—b	9—d	10—b
11—a	12—d	13—c	14—d	15—c
16—c	17—b	18—c	19—d	20—a

True-False

1—F	2—T	3—T	4—T	5—F
6—F	7—F	8—T	9—F	10—F
11—F	12—F	13—F	14—T	15—T

Fill in the blank

1—premises	2—Fourth	3—Fourteenth	4—elements
5—criminal	6—*corpus*	7—Substantive	8—felony
9—tort	10—*Actus*	11—Rights	12—innocence
13—plaintiff	14—Supreme	15—Constitution	

Chapter 3
FEDERAL COURTS

LEARNING OBJECTIVES

After reading this chapter, students should understand the
- basic principles of court organization.
- history of the federal courts.
- current four levels of the federal court system.
- function of specialized courts.
- administration of the federal judiciary.
- reasons for increasing caseloads in federal courts.
- consequences of federal involvement in the criminal justice system.

CHAPTER OUTLINE

I. **Basic Principles of Court Organization**
- A. Jurisdiction
  - 1. Geographical
  - 2. Subject matter
  - 3. Hierarchical
    - a. Original jurisdiction
    - b. Appellate jurisdiction
- B. Trial and Appellate Courts
- C. Dual Court System (state and federal)

II. **History of the Federal Courts**
- A. Constitutional Convention of 1787
- B. Judiciary Act of 1789-1891
- C. Court of Appeals Act of 1891
- D. Federal Courts Today

III. **U.S. Magistrate Judges**
  - 1. Nearly 499 magistrate judges (422 full-time and 77 Part-time)
  - 2. Perform quasi-judicial tasks to help alleviate district caseloads
- A. Caseload of Magistrate Judges
  - 1. Involved in about 494,000 felony and 100,000 misdemeanor matters annually

VI. **U.S. District Courts**
- A. Caseload of U.S. District Court
  - 1. Federal Questions
  - 2. Diversity Jurisdiction
  - 3. Prisoner Petitions
- B. U.S. Courts of Appeals
  - 1. Caseloads of U.S. Courts of Appeal

V.   U.S. Supreme Court
A.   Caseloads of the U.S. Supreme Court
1.   Selects which cases it will hear (rule of four)
2.   Decides about 80 cases a year

VI.   Specialized Courts
A.   Military Justice
B.   Military Non-combatants
C.   Foreign Intelligence Surveillance Court (FISA)

VII.   Federal Judicial Administration
A.   Chief Justice
B.   Judicial Conference of the United States
C.   Administrative Office of the U.S. Courts
D.   Federal Judicial Center
E.   Judicial Councils
F.   U.S. Sentencing Commission

VIII.   Rising Caseloads in the Federal Courts
A.   Over the last fifty years, district court filings have increased six fold
B.   In the same time, court of appeals cases have increased ten fold
C.   Increase the Number of Federal Judges
D.   Reduce Federal Jurisdiction

XI.   Consequences of Federal Involvement in the Criminal Justice System
A.   Limited Scope
B.   Forum for Symbolic Politics
C.   Federal Dollars

X.   Conclusion
1.   Crime will continue to be a major political issue
2.   Federal courts are a relatively small part of the nation's judicial system

KEY TERMS

appellate court - A court that hears appeals from trial courts on points of law. (54)

appellate jurisdiction - The authority of a court to hear, determine, and render judgment in an action on appeal from an inferior court. (53)

Article I - Section of the U.S. Constitution concerning the legislative branch of the national government. (64)

Article III - Section of the U.S. Constitution concerning the judicial branch of the national government. (56)

bankruptcy judge - Judicial officer who presides over the legal procedure under federal law by which a person is relieved of all debts after placing all property under the court's authority. An organization may be reorganized or terminated by the court in order to pay off creditors. (59)

constitutional courts - Federal courts created by Congress by virtue of its power under Article III of the Constitution to create courts inferior to the Supreme Court. (64)

district courts - U.S. trial courts established in the respective judicial districts into which the whole United States is divided. These courts are established for the purpose of hearing and deciding cases in limited districts to which their jurisdiction is confined. (59)

diversity of citizenship - When parties on the opposite sides of a federal lawsuit come from different states, the jurisdiction of the U.S. district courts can be invoked if the case involves a controversy concerning $75,000 or more in value. (60)

dual court system - A court system consisting of a separate judicial structure for each state in addition to a national structure. Each case is tried in a court of the same jurisdiction as that of the law or laws involved. (54)

en banc - French term referring to the session of an appellate court in which all the judges of the court participate, as opposed to a session presided over by three judges. (62)

extradition - Legal process whereby officials of one state surrender an alleged criminal offender to officials of the state in which the crime is alleged to have been committed. (52)

federal question - Case that contains a major issue involving the U.S. Constitution or U.S. laws or treaties. (60)

geographical jurisdiction - Geographical area over which courts can hear and decide disputes.(52)

hierarchical jurisdiction - Refers to differences in the functions of courts and involves original as opposed to appellate jurisdiction. (53)

jurisdiction - The power of a court to hear a case in question. (52)

legislative courts - Judicial bodies created by Congress under Article I (legislative article) and not Article III (judicial article). (64)

original jurisdiction - Jurisdiction in the first instance; commonly used to refer to trial jurisdiction as opposed to appellate jurisdiction. Appellate courts, however, have limited original jurisdiction. (53)

prisoner petition - Civil lawsuit filed by a prisoner alleging violations of his or her rights during trial or while in prison. (61)

subject matter jurisdiction - Types of cases courts have been authorized to hear and decide. (52)

trial court - Judicial body with primarily original jurisdiction in civil or criminal cases. Juries are used, and evidence is presented. (53)

U.S. magistrate judges - Judicial officers appointed by the U.S. district courts to perform the duties formerly performed by U.S. commissioners and to assist the court by serving as special masters in civil actions, conducting pretrial or discovery proceedings, and conducting preliminary review of applications for post-trial relief made by individuals convicted of criminal offenses. (57)

writ of certiorari - Order issued by an appellate court for the purpose of obtaining from a lower court the record of its proceedings in a particular case. (63)

CHAPTER SUMMARY

The three key concepts that are necessary to understand American judicial organization are jurisdiction, trial versus appellate courts, and the dual court system. Jurisdiction is the power of a court to decide a dispute. The three basic types of jurisdiction are geographical, subject matter and hierarchical. Geographical jurisdiction is based on geographical boundaries that follow the lines of governmental bodies such as cities, counties, states, etc. Extradition is the process in which one geographical jurisdiction surrenders a criminal to a different geographical jurisdiction were the crime was committed. Subject matter jurisdiction includes courts of limited jurisdiction, courts of general jurisdiction, traffic courts, and juvenile courts. Courts of limited jurisdiction are usually restricted to hearing misdemeanors and civil cases involving small amounts of money. Courts of general jurisdiction are empowered to hear all other types of cases within their jurisdiction.

Hierarchical jurisdiction refers to original jurisdiction and appellate jurisdiction. Courts of original jurisdiction have the authority to try and decide cases. Courts with appellate jurisdiction have the authority to review cases that have been decided by courts of original jurisdiction. In addition to the jurisdictional difference between trial and appellate courts, there are also many differences between the actual proceedings. While the purpose of trial courts is to hear disputes over facts, the primary task of appellate courts is to ensure that trial courts correctly interpret the law. Appellate courts engage in correcting errors made by lower courts and in making policy. In appellate courts, no witnesses are heard, no trials are conducted, and juries are never used. Furthermore, groups or panels of judges make appellate court decisions and often provide written reasons for their decisions, known as opinions.

America's dual court system can be quite complex. It consists of one national or federal court system and separate court systems for each of the fifty states. In essence, the framers of the U.S. Constitution created two parallel criminal justice systems. There are varying degrees of overlap as many crimes are covered by both state and federal law. Furthermore, parties in state courts may appeal to the U.S. Supreme Court or seek federal *habeas corpus*.

Article III of the U.S. Constitution called for a federal judiciary. It specifically mentioned a Supreme Court to settle disputes between states, and provided Congress with the ability to establish other courts as necessary. As a hotly debated topic between the Federalists and Anti-Federalists, Article III was the resulting compromise, a characteristic of the Constitutional Convention of 1787. After the Constitution was ratified, Federalists moved quickly to create lower federal courts. After extensive debate, the Judiciary Act of 1789 was passed. Although this act created lower federal courts, it was also a compromise, as the organization of the lower courts favored Anti-Federalists in that boundaries were drawn along state lines so that no district encompassed more than one state. According to the legislation, federal district judges were to be residents of their districts, and the lower federal courts were granted only limited jurisdiction.

The Judiciary Act of 1801 was a short-lived victory for the Federalists, as it created many new judgeships and extended the jurisdiction of the lower courts. However, after Thomas Jefferson was elected president, the Anti-Federalists quickly repealed the act and returned the federal judiciary to its former structure. The 1801 Act is best remembered for the resulting lawsuit of *Marbury v. Madison* in which Chief Justice Marshall created the power of judicial review, giving courts the ability to strike down unconstitutional acts of Congress.

The obvious inadequacy of the federal judicial system soon became apparent due to the hardships of circuit riding and increases in the appellate court caseload. Despite only minor modifications, the system remained largely unchanged for nearly a century. The Court of Appeals Act of 1891 represented a victory for the Federalists, as it created a circuit court of appeals to relieve the Supreme Court Justices of the need to ride the circuit. The Judges Bill passed in 1925, and congressional action in 1988 further eliminated mandatory appeals to the Supreme Court. Today, the Supreme Court has almost total control over its docket.

The current federal judiciary system is best described as having four layers: magistrate, district, appellate and the Supreme Court, with a plethora of specialized courts. U.S. magistrate judges are the federal equivalent of state trial court judges of limited jurisdiction and were created by Congress in 1968 to replace the former position of U.S. commissioners. Magistrates are assigned to help alleviate the increasing workload of district courts. Magistrate judges are selected by the district court judges and are Article I, not Article III judges. There are 422 full-time and 77 part-time magistrate judges. In felony cases, magistrates carry out preliminary proceedings such as initial appearances, preliminary hearings appointing counsel for indigents, setting of bail, and the issuing of search warrants. In misdemeanor and petty cases, magistrates may preside over trials, accept pleas of guilty and impose sentences. In civil cases, magistrate judges supervise discovery and may even conduct full trials with the consent of the litigants. Magistrate judges are involved in about 494,000 felony matters, over 100,000 misdemeanor and petty offenses and about 163,000 civil matters annually. Furthermore, magistrates review, but do not decide, over 30,000 prisoner petitions each year.

There are 94 U.S. district courts. There are 89 within the 50 states, one district court for the District of Columbia, and one territorial district court each for Guam, Puerto Rico, the Virgin Islands, and the Northern Mariana Islands. While some states may have more than one district court, no district court boundary crosses state lines. As some district courts cover large areas, they may be divided into subsections or divisions located in various locations throughout their respective districts. There are 678 district court judgeships. District judges are nominated by the President and must be confirmed by the Senate and serve for good behavior, which essentially means for life. There is one U.S. attorney in each district, whom unlike judges, serve at the pleasure of the president. District judges hear about 325,000 civil and criminal cases each year. Although drug prosecutions account for 29% of all federal criminal cases, civil lawsuits consume the majority of the federal court's time. Hearing about 55,000 each year, prisoner petitions constitute about 25% of the total civil caseload. District judges also hear cases involving a federal question or diversity of citizenship. There are also 352 bankruptcy judges, who are appointed by their respective courts of appeals. They serve 14-year terms and help alleviated district caseloads by hearing over 1.5 million petitions each year.

Created in 1891 and originally called Circuit Courts of Appeals, the Courts of Appeals system consists of twelve circuits. Eleven of the circuits are identified by number, while the twelfth is called the D.C. Circuit. The U.S. Courts of Appeals is staffed by 179 judges who are Article III judges. All Article III judges are nominated by the president and confirmed by the Senate. The courts of appeals normally utilize rotating three-judge panels, but may hear a case *en banc* with a majority vote. The U.S. Courts of Appeals hears approximately 57,000 cases annually, 20% of which come from criminal convictions of U.S. District Courts. Except for the small percentage of cases that make it to the U.S. Supreme Court, the Courts of Appeals are generally the courts of last resort for most federal litigation.

The nation's highest court, the Supreme Court, is made up of nine justices, eight associate and one chief justice, who is nominated specifically to that post by the president. Like other Article III judges, Supreme Court justices are nominated by the president, confirmed by the Senate and serve for good behavior. The Court reviews decisions from the U.S. Courts of Appeals and the state appellate courts of last resort, and also decides cases involving disputes between states. The Court employs the rule of four to select cases, in which four justices must vote to hear a case in order for it to be placed on the docket. The Court generally hears cases that involve a substantial federal question and decides only about eighty cases a year.

Specialized federal courts are created to hear specific types of cases, such as taxes, patents, or bankruptcy. Specialized courts, like U.S. magistrate judges and bankruptcy judges, are established by Congress under Article I of the U.S. Constitution and are thus known as legislative courts. While the majority of specialized courts are civil in nature, military courts and noncombatant proceedings deal with criminal matters. Congress designated Native American tribes as foreign nations in 1789 and thus encouraged self-government among the tribes. Due largely to the Indian Reorganization Act of 1934, there are 248 total tribal courts.

In 1950, Congress adopted the Uniform Code of Military Justice. This law provided new due process rights in courts martial, and created the U.S. Court of Appeals for the Armed Forces, which is composed of three civilian judges appointed for fifteen-year terms by the President. In addition to serving justice, military courts serve the additional purpose of enforcing order and discipline in the military. Military court proceedings differ from civilian courts in that proceedings are secret, rules of evidence are less demanding, six-person juries are used, the jurors are military personnel, a two-thirds majority vote is sufficient to convict and convictions are automatically appealed to a higher military court. As the U.S. military has decided that captured terrorists qualify as military non-combatants instead of prisoners of war, the Bush Administration has decided to try these military non-combatants in military courts where the proceedings will be secret and potential punishments include death. This stance taken by the Bush Administration has been hotly debated on both the national and international level. In 2006, Congress passed the Military Trials for Enemy Combatants Act, which allows the president to identify enemies, imprison them indefinitely, and interrogate them beyond the reach of the full court reviews traditionally afforded criminal defendants and ordinary prisoners.

In 1936, President Franklin Roosevelt attempted to expand the number of Supreme Court justices from nine to fifteen, allowing him to pack the Court with justices sympathetic to his policies. This legislation was not approved.

The Administrative Office Act of 1939 largely created the current administration of the federal judiciary. It established the Administrative Office of the U.S. Courts and judicial councils.

Today the Chief Justice is not only the presiding officer of the Supreme Court, but also the head of the federal judiciary system, which makes this position an *ex officio* member of several administrative organizations and provides the Chief Justice with the ability to appoint people to key administrative positions. The Judicial Conference of the United States is the administrative policy-making organization of the federal judicial system and is composed of the Chief Justice, chief judges of the courts of appeals, one district judge from each circuit and the chief judge of the Court of International Trade. As the Conference only meets semiannually for two-day sessions, most of the work is done by about twenty-five committees appointed by the Chief Justice. The Judicial Conference directs the Administrative Office in administering the budget, makes recommendations to Congress concerning judicial affairs, and plays a major role in the impeachment of federal judges.

The Administrative Office of the U.S. Courts has handled the daily tasks of the federal courts since 1939. The Director of the Administrative Office is appointed by the Chief Justice and the Office is responsible for lobbying, housekeeping, and accounting for the federal judiciary. The Federal Judicial Center is the research and training arm of the federal judiciary. It is headed by the Chief Justice, the Director of the Administrative Office and judges from the U.S. District Courts, U.S. Courts of Appeals and bankruptcy court. This organization's principal duty is the education and training of federal judges, probation officers, and court staff.
The judicial council or circuit council is the basic administrative unit of a circuit, consisting of both district and appellate judges. They are responsible for administering and monitoring the integrity of their respective circuits.

The U.S. Sentencing Commission is an independent agency in the judicial branch that was created by the Sentencing Reform Act of 1984. It is charged with developing federal sentencing guidelines. Today the Commission's duties have expanded to include making recommendations to Congress and research, evaluation, and development concerning sentencing issues.

Rising caseloads have been a fact of life for the federal judiciary since this nation's inception. However, in the last fifty years caseloads have been increasing alarmingly. District court filings have increased six fold and court of appeals cases have increased ten fold, partly due to the war on drugs. Two interesting dynamics come into play in this problem, both with deep historical roots. First, while in the past the number of federal judgeships has increased with rising caseloads, this is not the case today. Partisan politics in Congress will make it difficult to create and fill new judgeships. If the number of judgeships can't be increased, then the other popular option is to reduce federal jurisdiction, which is also unlikely due not only to political agendas, but also to a historical feud between this nation's lawmakers and law interpreters.

Although the public's fear of crime has become a hot topic and key campaign issue, in reality crime remains the responsibility of state and local governments. The dynamics of federal officials who want to be seen as doing something coupled with limited federal jurisdiction help explain the role of federal government in the criminal justice system. The federal government plays a limited role in justice, as the majority of crimes are violations of state law, not federal. Furthermore, the federal system has only 11% of the total law enforcement personnel, 10% of the total prison population and 7% of major trial court judges. Despite the above facts, the federal government remains the focal point for crime debate and has become the scene for various lobbyist groups, all pleading for favorable legislation. Congress is also pressed for funds to be used to fight crime, although the amount of federal dollars spent is small compared to the amount spent by local and state governments. In essence, Congress is asked to meet unlimited demands with limited resources as local and state agencies look to Washington for money.

While much of the public identifies the judiciary as a whole with federal courts, the reality is that federal courts are a relatively small part of America's judicial system. A major city like Chicago or Los Angeles prosecutes more felons in a year than the entire federal judiciary. Furthermore, state and local courts process the majority of street crimes, such as murder, rape, robbery and burglary. In contrast, federal crimes are often white collar or paper crimes like embezzlement or money laundering. Nevertheless, in an era where crime is a major political issue, we are unlikely to see a decrease in the federalization of state crimes.

PRACTICE TEST BANK

Multiple Choice

1. Native American matters of law are tried in _____.
    a. U.S. District Court
    b. U.S. Courts of Appeals
    c. U.S. Magistrate Courts
    d. tribal courts

2. Which of the following are not considered Article III judges?
    a. U.S. Magistrate judges
    b. U.S. District judges
    c. U.S. Courts of Appeals judges
    d. U.S. Supreme Court justices

3. Which of the following has almost total control over the cases it hears?
    a. U.S. Magistrate Courts
    b. U.S. District Courts
    c. U.S. Courts of Appeals
    d. U.S. Supreme Court

4. Which of the following is true of appellate courts?
    a. Witnesses are heard in appellate court cases.
    b. Juries are never used in appellate court.
    c. Single judges preside over appellate court proceedings.
    d. Appellate judges rarely write opinions.

5. Chief Justice Marshall created the power of judicial review in which case?
    a. *Mapp v. Ohio*
    b. *Marbury v. Madison*
    c. *Miranda v. Arizona*
    d. *Moussaoui v. U.S.*

6. How many people serve on a military court jury?
    a. 6
    b. 9
    c. 12
    d. 18

7. U.S. Magistrate judges are the federal equivalent of state _____.
    a. trial court judges of limited jurisdiction
    b. trial court judges of general jurisdiction
    c. appellate court judges
    d. supreme court judges

8.   How many justices serve on the U.S. Supreme Court?
        a.   6
        b.   7
        c.   9
        d.   12

9.   In 1937, which president's plan to pack the Supreme Court was defeated?
        a.   Theodore Roosevelt
        b.   Richard Nixon
        c.   Harry S. Truman
        d.   Franklin D. Roosevelt

10.   How many districts are in the U.S. District Court system?
        a.   64
        b.   94
        c.   123
        d.   450

11.   In deciding to grant certiorari to hear a case, the Supreme Court depends on _____.
        a.   the rule of five
        b.   a majority vote
        c.   the rule of four
        d.   the rule of thumb

12.   What type of cases is considered the backbone of U.S. Court of Appeals workload?
        a.   death penalty cases
        b.   civil cases
        c.   habeas corpus cases
        d.   juvenile cases

13.   The dual court system refers to _____.
        a.   trial and appellate courts
        b.   federal and state courts
        c.   civil and criminal law
        d.   bench and jury trials

14.   Which Article of the U.S. Constitution provides an outline for the federal judiciary?
        a.   Article I
        b.   Article II
        c.   Article III
        d.   Article IV

15. Original and appellate jurisdiction fall under what classification of jurisdiction?
    a. geographical jurisdiction
    b. subject matter jurisdiction
    c. hierarchical jurisdiction
    d. general jurisdiction

16. The U.S. Court of Appeals is made up of how many judgeships?
    a. 9
    b. 79
    c. 179
    d. 680

17. To restrict minor disputes in federal court, in 1996 Congress raised the amount in controversy in civil disputes to _____.
    a. $10,000
    b. $25,000
    c. $75,000
    d. $100,000

18. Article III judges serve _____.
    a. 4-year terms
    b. 8-year terms
    c. at the will of the President
    d. for good behavior, which is essentially life

19. The Chief Justice of the Supreme Court does not play a role in which of the following?
    a. Judicial Conference of the United States
    b. Administrative Office of the U.S. Courts
    c. U.S. Sentencing Commission
    d. Federal Judicial Center

20. Judicial bodies created by Congress under Article I are commonly referred to as _____.
    a. courts of limited jurisdiction
    b. courts of general jurisdiction
    c. constitutional courts
    d. legislative courts

True-False

1. Criminal cases consume more federal courts time than civil lawsuits.
    a. true
    b. false

2. Federal magistrates can try and sentence felony defendants.
   a. true
   b. false

3. The Federal Judicial Center is responsible for developing federal sentencing guidelines.
   a. true
   b. false

4. Congress adopted the Uniform Code of Military Justice in 1950.
   a. true
   b. false

5. In most cases, in the federal system, the Court of Appeals is generally the court of last resort.
   a. true
   b. false

6. Drug prosecutions account for about 29% of all federal criminal cases.
   a. true
   b. false

7. Article III judges are nominated by the Senate, but must be confirmed by the president.
   a. true
   b. false

8. Justices for the U.S. Court of Appeals for the Armed Forces are civilians.
   a. true
   b. false

9. U.S. magistrate judges are appointed by district court judges.
   a. true
   b. false

10. Prisoner petitions make up about 25% of the federal civil caseload.
    a. true
    b. false

11. Federal magistrate judges may only conduct civil trials with consent from the litigants.
    a. true
    b. false

12. U.S. District court jurisdictions may often encompass more than one state.
    a. true
    b. false

13. A major city like Chicago or Los Angeles prosecutes more felons in a year than the entire federal judiciary.
    a.   true
    b.   false

14. The majority of events labeled as crime are violations of federal law, not state law.
    a.   true
    b.   false

15. Some states may have more than one federal district court.
    a.   true
    b.   false

Fill in the Blank

1. Captured terrorists have recently been declared military _____ instead of prisoners of war.

2. The U.S. Supreme Court hears and decides about _____ cases each year.

3. There is/are _____ U.S. attorney/s for each district.

4. The legal process in which officials of one state or country surrender a criminal offender to another is known as _____.

5. In the late 1700s, advocates for strong national government were known as Nationalists or _____.

6. Federal courts inferior to the Supreme Court and created by Congress under Article III are commonly referred to as _____ courts.

7. *En* _____ is the French term referring to the session of an appellate court in which all judges participate.

8. A _____ *of certiorari* is issued by appellate courts to obtain and review the proceedings of a lower court.

9. In 2003, the Bush administration decided that military noncombatants should be tried in military courts where the proceedings would be _____.

10. The Foreign Intelligence Surveillance Act is commonly known as _____.

11. Diversity of _____ cases involves suits between citizens of different states or between a U.S. citizen and a foreign country or citizen.

12.   In 1789, congress designated Native American tribes as foreign _____.

13.   The power of a court to hear a case is known as _____.

14.   A case that contains a major issue involving the U.S. Constitution or U.S. laws or treaties is known as a case involving a _____ question.

15.   Two popular options to deal with rising federal caseloads are to _____ federal judgeships or to reduce federal jurisdiction.

Essay

1.   What are the four levels of judges in the federal court system? Describe their duties.

2.   Explain the history of the Federalists/Anti-Federalists debate and how it has affected the judiciary over the years.

3.   Trace the steps in a federal felony case from the U.S. Magistrate Judges to the U.S. Supreme Court. Briefly describe what happens at each step.

4.   What are the differences between constitutional courts and legislative courts and judges?

5.   Describe the two major options for dealing with rising federal caseloads. What are some of the difficulties in implementing these options?

CHAPTER 3 ANSWER KEY

Multiple Choice

1—d	2—a	3—d	4—b	5—b
6—a	7—a	8—c	9—d	10—b
11—c	12—b	13—b	14—c	15—c
16—c	17—c	18—d	19—c	20—d

True-False

1—F	2—F	3—F	4—F	5—T
6—T	7—F	8—T	9—T	10—T
11—T	12—F	13—T	14—F	15—T

Fill in the blank

1—non-combatant	2—80	3—one	4—extradition
5—Federalists	6—constitutional	7—*banc*	8—*writ*
9—secret	10—FISA	11—citizenship	12—nations
13—jurisdiction	14—federal	15—increase	

Chapter 4
STATE COURTS

LEARNING OBJECTIVES

After reading this chapter, students should understand the

- impact of England on our early history of state courts.
- limited jurisdiction of lower courts.
- role of major trial courts.
- function of intermediate courts of appeals.
- function of state supreme courts.
- centralized unification of the state court system.
- emerging reform agenda for courts.
- consequences of court organization.

CHAPTER OUTLINE

I. **History of State Courts**
    A. Colonial Courts
    B. Early American Courts
    C. Courts in a Modernizing Society

II. **Trial Courts of Limited Jurisdiction: Lower Courts**
    A. Trial courts of limited jurisdiction

III. **Trial Courts of General Jurisdiction: Major Trial Courts**
    A. Trial courts of general jurisdiction
    B. Criminal Cases
    C. Civil Cases

IV. **Intermediate Courts of Appeals**
    A. Regional vs. statewide
    B. Some courts hear both criminal and civil cases, while some states have a bifurcated system.

V. **Courts of Last Resort: State Supreme Courts**
    A.. Criminal/civil vs. bifurcated system
    B. Docket discretion varies between states

VI. **Court Unification**
    A. Key Components
        1. Simplified court structure
        2. Centralized administration
        3. Centralized rule making
        4. Centralized judicial budgeting and statewide financing
    B. Analysis

VII. Problem-Solving Courts
    A.   Therapeutic jurisprudence
        1.   Immediate intervention
        2.   Nonadversarial adjudication
        3.   Treatment programs with clear rules and structured goals
        4.   A team approach of judge, prosecutors, defense counsel, treatment providers and correctional staff
    B.   Drug Courts
    C.   Domestic Violence Courts

VIII. Consequences of Court Organization
    A.   Decentralization and choice of courts
    B.   Local Control and Local Corruption.

IX. Conclusion

KEY TERMS

domestic relations - Relating to the home; the law of divorce, custody, support, adoption, and so on. (83)

drug courts - Specialty courts with jurisdiction over cases involving illegal substances. Drug courts typically stress treatment rather than punishment. (92)

estate - The interest a person has in property; a person's right or title to property. (83)

intermediate courts of appeals (ICAs) - Judicial bodies falling between the highest, or supreme, tribunal and the trial court; created to relieve the jurisdiction's highest court of hearing a large number of cases. (85)

personal injury - Negligence lawsuits, often involving automobile accidents. (83)

state supreme court - General term for the highest court in a state. (85)

therapeutic jurisprudence - Judicial bodies such as drug courts that stress helping defendants in trouble through nonadversarial proceedings. (92)

trial court of general jurisdiction - A trial court responsible for major criminal and civil cases.(82)

trial court of limited jurisdiction - A lower-level state court, such as a justice of the peace court, whose jurisdiction is limited to minor civil disputes or misdemeanors. (82)

unified court system - A simplified state trial court structure with rule making centered in the supreme court, system governance authority vested in the chief justice of the supreme court, and state funding of the judicial system under a statewide judicial budget. (90)

CHAPTER SUMMARY

Based on English common law, early colonial American courts were rather simple compared to the complex English court system. As towns and courts grew, courts systems also grew to adapt to the changes induced by growing populations. County courts stood at the heart of American colonial government, often holding legislative, judicial and executive powers. Soon the idea of a separation of governmental powers began to emerge.

Diversity was the hallmark of the colonies, as their courts reflected variations in local customs, geography, religious practices and commerce. Much of this variety is still evident in the court systems of the U.S. today. Colonial courts fell out of favor after the American Revolution. Judicial power was absorbed by legislative bodies due to colonists' distrust of lawyers and English common law. As Americans were not anxious to see the development of a large, independent judiciary, state legislatures often responded to unpopular court decisions by removing judges or abolishing courts altogether. A major source of conflict between legislatures and courts centered around finance. Legislators were more responsive to policies that favored debtors, while the courts were more responsive to the interests of creditors, such as merchants. Eventually, however, courts emerged as independent political institutions.

Rapid industrialization, urbanization and population increases after the Civil War spurred the largest judicial growth and changes in U.S. history. Still reflecting the rural agrarian society of the early 19th century, courts were unable to meet the rising demands of urbanization. A new type of social problem, crimes committed by juveniles, emerged at the end of the 19th century. States and localities responded to increased demands by creating city courts to deal with public disturbances such as gambling and prostitution. They also created specialty courts to deal with specific cases like small claims and family relations.

The sporadic and unplanned expansion of the American courts systems resulted in a complex and confusing structure. Chicago justice of the peace courts allowed defendants to court shop for the court that would offer them the most political and legal advantages. Furthermore, the structure of these courts did not allow an avenue for overloaded courts to shift some of their caseload to the less-burdened. Such courts also produced political patronage jobs for the city's political machines.

Contrary to popular belief, state courts, not federal, try the majority of cases, both civil and criminal. The structure of most state court systems can best be understood as having four levels: trial courts of limited jurisdiction, trial courts of general jurisdiction, intermediate courts of appeals, and courts of last resort. While some states do not possess all four levels, this is the basic structure of state court systems.

There are over 13,500 trial courts of limited jurisdiction in the U.S. staffed by over 18,000 judicial officers. These courts account for 85% of all judicial bodies in the U.S. and are often referred to as inferior courts or lower courts. The number of lower courts varies from none in some states to nearly 3,000 in others. Most of these courts are created by city or county government and are therefore not part of the state judiciary. They are locally controlled and funded. Inferior courts are variously called justice, justice of the peace, city, magistrate, or municipal courts. Lower courts handle over 61 million matters a year, the majority of which are traffic cases (41 million). These are the courts that most citizens will face. As trial courts of limited jurisdiction, these courts are limited to hearing misdemeanor, traffic, and small claims cases, and sometimes the preliminary stages of felony cases.

At the second level, there are an estimated 2,000 trial courts of general jurisdiction, staffed by over 11,000 judges. While generally referred to as major trial courts, the most common names for these courts are district, circuit, or superior. The geographical boundaries of major trial courts are defined along existing political boundaries, primarily counties. Major trial courts have the authority to hear all matters not specifically delegated to lower courts. In most states, the trial courts of general jurisdiction are grouped into judicial districts or circuits. In rural areas these districts may encompass several adjoining counties. In such rural districts, judges hear a wide variety of cases as they ride circuit, holding court in different counties within their district. Heavily populated counties have only one circuit or district for the area and judges are often specialists assigned to hear only certain types of cases. Thirty-one million cases are filed each year in the nation's state trial courts, more than eighty times the number of similar filings in the federal district court.

The types of cases filed in state and federal courts differ greatly. While litigants in federal court are most often big business and governmental bodies, litigants in state courts are typically individuals and small businesses. While federal courts hear a large percentage of white-collar crime and drug distribution cases, state courts decide primarily street crimes. The more serious criminal violations are heard in trial courts of general jurisdiction. While the public associates felonies with violent crime, the reality is that 90% of criminal violations involve nonviolent crimes. Perhaps the fastest growing types of cases heard by state courts are drug cases. Over the last decade and a half, criminal cases filed in general jurisdiction courts (primarily felonies) have increased 25%. As the majority of criminal cases do not go to trial, the dominant issue in major trial courts is not guilt or innocence, but what penalty to apply.

While criminal cases are often highly publicized, civil cases dominate the dockets of major trial courts. Contrary to popular belief, domestic relations cases, not personal injury, are the single largest category of cases filed in the major trial courts. Domestic matters account for a full one third of total case filings and are the fastest growing part of the civil caseload. Estate cases, often referred to as probate, involve the disbursement of a deceased's assets and are the second most common type of case filed in the state's major trial courts. Most estate cases raise little if any controversy for judges. Personal injury cases constitute the third most common type of case filings in state and trial courts of general jurisdiction, the majority of which involve automobile accidents. While such tort cases only account for 8% of all filings in trial courts, they are the most likely to go to trial. Contrary to popular belief, most tort cases involve small settlements and tort case filings have been steadily declining since 1996. State major trial courts try a plethora of civil cases, including contract cases, debt collection, and property rights.

Intermediate courts of appeals, or ICAs, came to fruition to help relieve an overwhelming growth of appellate cases going to state supreme courts. Today, thirty-nine states have intermediate appellate courts. Those who don't are sparsely populated and have a low volume of appeals. While ICAs must hear all properly filed appeals (mandatory appellate jurisdiction), subsequent appeals are at the discretion of the higher court (discretionary jurisdiction). Thus, a decision by the state's intermediate appellate court is the final one for the majority of cases, as relatively few make it to the Supreme Court level. Currently, twenty-four states organize their ICAs on a statewide basis, while the rest are organized on a regional basis. While these bodies in most states hear both civil and criminal cases, Alabama and Tennessee have separate courts of intermediate appeals for civil and criminal cases. Like their federal counterparts, these courts usually employ rotating three-judge panels to decide cases.

Because ICAs handle the bulk of the appellate caseload, many states have had to add judgeships to keep up with rising caseloads. However, many ICAs face the same workload problems today that spawned their existence. Criminal defendants who are increasingly likely to appeal their convictions with free attorneys often find appellate courts to be unsympathetic to their legal argument. Only one in sixteen criminal defendants who appeals receives a major victory.

The courts of last resort, or supreme courts, are the highest state courts and generally hear all cases *en banc*. While most state courts of last resort have discretionary jurisdiction, much like the Supreme Court, high courts in states without an intermediate court of appeal have little discretion in their docket. Interestingly, Texas and Oklahoma have two courts of last resort, one for civil appeals and one for criminal appeals. While litigants may pursue an appeal from a state court of last resort to the U.S. Supreme Court, few are successful in getting their case heard. Like the U.S. Supreme Court, state courts of last resort often decide issues that have a major impact on the law and government of their jurisdiction.

Historically, court reform has been associated with implementing a unified court system due to the disorganization and inefficiencies of many state courts. The main goal of a unified court system is to shift judicial administration from local control to centralized management. This would concentrate authority in the state capital instead of within a loose network of judges. Reformers have come up with five general principles for court reform: a simplified, uniform court structure, centralized administration, centralized budgeting, centralized rule making, and statewide financing. A three-tier system is envisioned, which would consist of a state supreme court, intermediate courts of appeal, and a single trial court. Such a unified system would shift control from legislatures to judges and lawyers and also allow for a single state judiciary budget with adequate financing for all state courts.

However, opponents of court reform believe that such a system would lack the diversity necessary to mete out justice in locations as different as rural and urban areas inhabited by starkly different people with different beliefs. Critics also argue that such reforms stress abstract ideas of court organization (law on the books) instead of the realities of the courthouse (law in action), and are thus unresponsive to the realities of normal cases heard in the nation's courts. Today court reform has come to concentrate more on efficiency than on neat organizational structures, as is evident in the proliferation of specialized courts.

Initially called designer courts or boutique courts, specialized or specialty courts such as drug courts, family courts, drunk-driving courts, and others have been created. The five essential elements of therapeutic justice are: immediate intervention, nonadversarial adjudication, hands-on judicial involvement, treatment programs with clear rules and structured goals, and a team approach that brings together the judge, prosecutors, defense counsel, treatment provider, correctional staff and others involved. Drug treatment courts are the best-known examples of therapeutic jurisprudence.

The emergence of drug courts is largely due to effects of the Drug War, in which drug arrests have become the single most dominant police activity. However, the case backlog is not as bad as officials first feared, due to the straightforward nature of drug cases, in which a guilty plea is usually entered shortly after arraignment and due in part to the existence of drug courts. Generally drug courts emphasize treatment based on the philosophy that treatment will reduce the recidivism of drug offenders. To be eligible for such treatment programs, defendants must have no prior felony convictions, must be charged with possession only, and must admit their drug problem and request treatment. Early evaluations have shown favorable but not phenomenal success and generally result in lower recidivism.

As a result of the complexities of the decentralized American legal systems, lawyers sometimes try to maneuver cases so that they are heard in courts perceived to be favorable to their clients. Furthermore, many offenses violate both state and federal laws, in which case federal officials usually prosecute major violations and state officials prosecute minor cases.

While many of the state court systems are not funded or controlled on a local basis, the judges, prosecutors and defense attorneys reside in these same communities, adding local flavor to the application of state law. However, such local control has also been known to be conducive to corruption and injustice. Nevertheless, the dual court system acts as a safety valve for unchecked abuses of justice, as it is often federal, not state officials who prosecute local officials.

Despite the many types of court reform proposed, today's court reform is marked by tremendous experimentation at the local level and a focus on efficiency. While not set up along the clean organizational lines that reformers envisioned, judges and court actors have the ability to adapt and use local resources at their disposal to keep the cases moving. This ability to adapt to change has long been a hallmark of the American judiciary.

PRACTICE TEST BANK

Multiple Choice

1.   A person contesting a traffic ticket would most likely appear in _____.
     a.   a court of general jurisdiction
     b.   a court of limited jurisdiction
     c.   a court of intermediate appeals
     d.   a court of last resort

2.   The majority of inferior court cases are _____.
     a.   civil cases
     b.   public order cases
     c.   ordinance violations
     d.   traffic offenses

3.   About how many criminal defendants will receive a major victory upon appeal?
     a.   one in six
     b.   one in sixteen
     c.   one in thirty-six
     d.   one in sixty

4.   Intermediate courts of appeals typically employ _____.
     a.   single-judge panels
     b.   rotating three-judge panels
     c.   rotating five-judge panels
     d.   nine-judge panels

5.   To be eligible for treatment by drug courts, defendants _____.
     a.   must have a prior felony conviction
     b.   must not have a prior misdemeanor conviction
     c.   must be charged with sale only
     d.   must admit their drug problem

6.   Which of the following is true of locally-controlled justice?
     a.   It creates more rights for local citizens.
     b.   It prevents corruption.
     c.   It creates a boundary between the courts and the citizens.
     d.   It can be an incubator for injustice.

7.   Which of the following is not a trial court of general jurisdiction?
     a.   superior court
     b.   circuit court
     c.   justice of the peace court
     d.   district court

8. Which of the following is not an element of therapeutic jurisprudence?
    a. immediate intervention
    b. nonadversarial adjudication
    c. hands-on judicial involvement
    d. centralized administration

9. Which type of case constitutes the largest category of cases filed in major trial courts?
    a. domestic relations
    b. estate
    c. criminal
    d. personal injury

10. Which of the following is a general principle of a unified court system?
    a. a complex court structure
    b. decentralized rule making
    c. local financing
    d. centralized administration

11. Which of the following states have intermediate courts of appeals to hear civil and criminal cases separately?
    a. Texas and Oklahoma
    b. California and New York
    c. Alabama and Tennessee
    d. California and Texas

12. After the American Revolution, the power of state courts was drastically reduced and taken over by _____.
    a. Congress
    b. state legislatures
    c. state governors
    d. the federal judiciary

13. There are over how many trial courts of limited jurisdiction in the U.S.?
    a. 2,000
    b. 8,000
    c. 13,500
    d. 35,000

14. Of all cases filed in major trial courts, tort cases are the most likely to _____.
    a. end in a settlement
    b. be appealed
    c. be settled before trial
    d. go to trial

15. Most trial courts of limited jurisdiction are funded and operated _____.
    a. locally
    b. by the state
    c. by the federal judiciary
    d. by the state legislatures

16. Litigants may appeal from their state's court of last resort to the _____.
    a. U.S. Magistrates
    b. U.S. District Court
    c. U.S. Courts of Appeals
    d. U.S. Supreme Court

17. There are approximately how many trial courts of general jurisdiction in the U.S?
    a. 200
    b. 2,000
    c. 13,500
    d. 35,000

18. Lower courts constitute what percentage of all judicial bodies in the United States?
    a. 15%
    b. 25%
    c. 60%
    d. 85%

19. In states with intermediate appellate courts, state supreme courts _____.
    a. have complete discretion in the cases placed on their dockets
    b. have little discretion in the cases placed on their dockets
    c. hear only civil cases
    d. hear only criminal cases

20. Which of the following states have two courts of last resort?
    a. Alabama and Tennessee
    b. Alabama and Texas
    c. New York and California
    d. Oklahoma and Texas

True-False

1. In addition to hearing misdemeanors and traffic cases, trial courts of limited jurisdiction also conduct the preliminary stages of felony cases.
    a. true
    b. false

2. Most drug cases are straightforward, as pleas of guilty are entered shortly after arraignment.
    a.   true
    b.   false

3. In colonial America, local government often held executive, legislative, and judicial powers.
    a.   true
    b.   false

4. The average citizen is most likely to come into contact with trial courts of general jurisdiction.
    a.   true
    b.   false

5. Today court reform concentrates more on providing a neater organization for the justice system than on specialty courts and backlog.
    a.   true
    b.   false

6. In discussing court reform and unification, reformers generally envision a three-tier system.
    a.   true
    b.   false

7. Trial courts of limited jurisdiction are generally created by city or county governments.
    a.   true
    b.   false

8. The most common type of civil case heard by major trial courts involves personal injury.
    a.   true
    b.   false

9. State and local courts derive their power from Article III of the U.S. Constitution.
    a.   true
    b.   false

10. In states without intermediate appellate courts, state supreme courts have complete discretion in the cases placed on their dockets.
    a.   true
    b.   false

11. Most criminal cases go to trial.
    a.   true
    b.   false

12. For the majority of cases, a decision by a state's intermediate appellate court is final.
    a. true
    b. false

13. The court systems of each state are made up of four levels.
    a. true
    b. false

14. Tort case filings have been increasing since 1996.
    a. true
    b. false

15. Intermediate courts of appeals engage primarily in error correction to make sure the law has been followed by the lower courts.
    a. true
    b. false

Fill in the Blank

1. By the end of the 19th century, the nation had to respond to a new type of social problem; crimes committed by _____.

2. There are approximately 2,000 trial courts of _____ jurisdiction in the U.S.

3. Litigants in state court are most often individuals and _____ businesses.

4. Trial courts of limited jurisdiction are often referred to as _____ courts or inferior courts.

5. The _____ jurisdictions of major trial courts are defined along political boundaries, primarily counties.

6. Centralized budgeting and administration are two characteristics of court _____.

7. After the American Revolution, colonists distrusted _____ and English common law.

8. The local control of justice has often been the incubator for corruption and _____.

9. In addition to hearing misdemeanor and traffic cases, trial courts of limited jurisdiction also conduct the _____ stages of felony cases.

10. Courts of last resort are commonly known as _____ courts.

11. Drug treatment courts are the best-known examples of _____ jurisprudence.

12. Trial courts of general jurisdiction are commonly known as _____ trial courts.

13. The principal objective of a unified court system is to shift judicial administration from local control to _____ management.

14. The _____ court system has provided a safety valve for checking the most flagrant abuses of local justice.

15. State courts receive over _____ times the number of filings received by federal district courts.

Essay

1. Explain the rationale for and list the five general principles of court unification.

2. What is therapeutic jurisprudence? What are its five elements?

3. Discuss the advantages and disadvantages of court unification.

4. Discuss the general structure of the state court system.

5. Discuss the advantages and rationale for a bifurcated judiciary.

CHAPTER 4 ANSWER KEY

Multiple Choice

1—b	2—d	3—b	4—b	5—d
6—d	7—c	8—d	9—a	10—d
11—c	12—b	13—c	14—d	15—a
16—d	17—b	18—d	19—a	20—d

True-False

1—T	2—T	3—T	4—F	5—F
6—T	7—T	8—F	9—F	10—F
11—F	12—T	13—F	14—F	15—T

Fill in the Blank

1.—juveniles	2—general	3—small	4—lower
5—geographical	6—unification	7—lawyers	8—injustice
9—preliminary	10—supreme	11—therapeutic	12—major
13—centralized	14—dual	15—eighty	

Chapter 5
THE DYNAMICS OF COURTHOUSE JUSTICE

LEARNING OBJECTIVES
After reading this chapter, students should understand the
- nature and design of courthouses.
- role of various courthouse workers.
- dynamics of courthouse justice.
- assembly-line justice process.
- function of discretionary decisions.
- role of the courtroom work group.
- problem and consequences of delay.
- law-on-the books and law-in-action approach to court delay.

CHAPTER OUTLINE

I. **The Courthouse and the People Who Work There**
    A.   The Courthouse
    B.   The Courtroom
    C.   Behind the Scenes

II. **Dynamics of the Courthouse**
    A.   Expectations

III. **Assembly-Line Justice**
    A.   Strengths of the Explanation
    B.   Weakness of the Explanation

IV. **Discretion**
    A.   Discretion has three major subcomponents:
        1.   Legal judgments
        2.   Policy priorities
        3.   Personal philosophies

V. **The Courtroom Work Group**
    A.   Mutual Interdependence
        1.   Members
            a.   Judges
            b.   Prosecuting attorneys
            c.   Defense attorneys (private or public defenders)
    B.   Shared Decision Making
    C.   Socialization
    D.   Normal Crimes
    E.   Rewards and Sanctions
    F.   Variability in Courtroom Work Groups

VI.   Legal Ethics
A.   Morals and conflict with legal ethics

VII.   The Problem of Delay
A.   Consequences of Delay
1.   Jeopardizes defendant's right to a speedy trial.
2.   Erodes public confidence in the judicial process.
B.   Assessing the Costs of Delay

VIII.   Law-on-the-Books Approach to Court Delay
A.   Speedy-Trial Laws
1.   Federal speedy Trial Law of 1974 (amended in 1979)
2.   Exists in all 50 states
3.   Designed to protect defendants' rights
B.   Limits of Speedy-Trial Laws
1.   Varying impact on case flow
a.   Federal laws have proven effective.
b.   State laws fail to provide resources and monitoring.

XI.   Law-in-Action Approach to Court Delay
A.   Case Scheduling
B.   Efforts at Coordination

X.   Conclusion
A.   Excessive caseloads do not always explain delay.
B.   Discretion gives actors flexibility.
C.   Courtroom workgroup norms largely determine courtroom speed.

KEY TERMS

assembly-line justice - The operation of any segment of the criminal justice system in which excessive workload results in decisions being made with such speed and impersonality that defendants are treated as objects to be processed rather than as individuals. (105)

clerk of court - An elected or appointed court officer responsible for maintaining the written records of the court and for supervising or performing the clerical tasks necessary to conduct judicial business. (102)

courtroom work group - The regular participants in the day-to-day activities of a particular courtroom; judge, prosecutor, and defense attorney interacting on the basis of shared norms.(108)

delay - Postponement or adjournment of proceedings in a case; lag in case-processing time. (113)

normal crime - Categorization of crime based on the typical manner in which it is committed, the type of defendant who typically commits it, and the typical penalty to be applied. (109)

routine administration - A matter that presents the court with no disputes over law or fact. (107)

CHAPTER SUMMARY

The realities of courthouse justice highlight the differences between the law in action and the law on the books. To many Americans, the courthouse is the embodiment of justice, a concrete and tangible symbol of our ideals of law and order. Although criminal courthouses are constructed in a wide variety of architectural styles, they nevertheless all seem to present an image of stolidity and unyielding strength. While courthouses may vary in size, they are all basically the same in design.

While basically the same, one will notice small differences between small and large courthouses. Generally in a small courthouse, one finds only a handful of courthouse regulars who handle many different types of criminal and civil cases. In contrast, one will find numerous courthouse regulars who specialize in specific duties in large courthouses. Many of the courtroom regulars like lawyers and bail bondsmen spend so much time in the courthouse, that the hallways are said to be their daytime offices. Nevertheless, the courthouse depends on a wide variety of both lawyers and nonlawyers to perform their vital roles in the daily orchestration of our justice system. Of course, the majority of this happens in the courtroom.

Most courtrooms are set up in the same fashion. The judge sits on a raised platform behind the bench at the head of the court. Usually the clerk of court or calendar clerk controls the scheduling of cases and keeps the judge apprised of such matters. Similarly, somewhere near the bench will be the court stenographer or court reporter that makes a shorthand record of the proceedings. The bailiff, who tries to maintain order in the courtroom, generally is located at the front of the court as may be the judge's law clerk.

The tables for the prosecution and defense are generally located about ten to twenty feet in front of the bench. While the public defender may temporarily give up his seat to a private attorney, the public defender's files remains, an indication of the public defender's regularity and position in court. The podium is generally located between the bench and the lawyers' tables. However, the podium is only used for ceremonial occasions, such as the entering of a plea by the defendant or by the lawyers when arguing before the jury. Otherwise, lawyers typically argue while sitting behind their respective tables. The jury box is located to one side of the bench and is occupied by the jury members in such a trial. However, in absence of a jury trial, a variety of people can be found occupying this area waiting, socializing, or conducting business. Other courtroom regulars include police officers as witnesses, probation officers, substance abuse counselors, pretrial service representatives, and bail agents. Defendants out on bail sit in the public sector, while detainees are guarded by a number of deputies. The number of deputies guarding the detainees is a good indicator of the perceived threat of the defendants.

A railing separates the courthouse regulars from the occasional participants, with the first couple of rows usually being reserved for lawyers. Besides family and friends, observers and interest groups can also be found sitting in the public sector. Spectators in the courtroom are quick to notice that the actors are always in motion and that the cast of characters is ever changing.

Courts are paperwork bureaucracies. As even the simplest cases require sheets upon sheets of paperwork, much of this paperwork is created and processed behind the scenes. While the actions of these behind the scene actors are hardly ever visible, their failures can make headlines.

A common complaint about courtroom efficiency is that courts are mismanaged. Part of this problem arises from the existence of three distinct types of court managers who are often in competition with one another: clerks of court, chief judges, and court administrators. This competition is based on the fundamental conflict between management and the law profession or the rationality of bureaucracy versus the anti-bureaucratic philosophies of judges.

The clerk of court, also referred to as prothonotary, register of probate, or clerk, is responsible for docketing cases, collecting fees, overseeing jury selection, and maintaining court records. Clerks of court are elected officials in all but six states, and therefore can operate semi-autonomously from the judge, creating a traditional competition for control of judicial administration.

While judges are responsible for court, they have most often been ineffective managers. Judges are not trained in management and are often found to be lacking the managerial skills and necessary authority to totally control the courthouse. As chief judges are generally chosen by seniority, they are considered first among equals, and such a meritorious position is not a guarantee of the judge's effective management skills.

Professionals trained in managerial skills and bureaucratic knowledge have become commonplace in courthouses under the title of court manager or court administrator. The primary duties of court administrators are to prepare annual reports, summarize caseload data, prepare budgets, and perform troubleshooting. By the 1980s every state had a court administrator, who would report to the state supreme court or chief justice. Trial courts have also begun to use court administrators and today, few if any large cities can be found without court administrators.

There is really no clear distinction between the administration and adjudication. This leaves much room for tension and disagreement between court administrators and judges.
Many first time court observers are shocked to find that courtroom dynamics resemble little of the popular images instilled by the popular media. Observers will find fast paced disposition of dockets along with discretion in a very non-adversarial atmosphere. Scholars have employed three concepts to study the differences between the law on the books and the law in action: assembly-line justice, discretion, and the courtroom work group.

Every year, about fourteen million people are arrested by police, three million of which are for felonies. Due to the large volume of cases and shortage of judges, prosecutors and other personnel in some courts, judicial officials are more interested in expediency and efficiency than in individually trying each case. "Assembly line justice" is the term to describe the ensuing mass-production techniques of processing defendants through the court system. Group processing and the use of specialized attorneys for each stage of processing are two such techniques.

Assembly line justice is the most common reason given for why courts do not administer justice by the textbook image. In general, American courts have suffered from overloaded dockets for over a century. Furthermore, while plea bargaining is thought to be a recent invention, plea bargaining actually predates many of today's modern court problems. Plea bargaining began in the early nineteenth century and became a standard feature in American courthouses by 1900.

Emphasizing heavy caseloads and the mass production techniques used to deal with them often fails to take into account that the majority of cases are routine and have little dispute over fact or law. As such cases usually end in a plea of guilty before trial, routine administration allows the courts to effectively process such clear-cut cases. A study of two Connecticut courts, one with a heavy caseload and another with a light workload found that justice was actually handled the same, and that the courts had amazingly similar practices. The only real difference was that the court with the heavier workload was in session longer to hear the greater number of cases.

While the law on the books view of our legal system projects an image of an infallible adversary system with infinite resources, the law in action approach, which focuses on a limited number of resources and discretion, is much more realistic. Discretion lies at the heart of the criminal justice system. It is exercised at every point in the criminal justice process. Discretion has three major subcomponents: legal judgments, policy priorities, and personal philosophies. The courtroom work group is a collective name for the regular actors in a given courtroom, specifically the judge and attorneys. Members of the courtroom work group develop a commonality of trust and cooperation through working together on a daily basis in order to expeditiously and efficiently dispose of cases. There are basically five characteristics of the courtroom work group: mutual interdependence, shared decision making, socialization, normal crimes, and rewards and sanctions.

The courtroom is not a single organization, but depends on a collection of representatives from different institutions to run effectively. As none of the actors can truly make decisions or act independently, they must work together and consider the actions and reactions of other members of the work group. Working together is in the best interest of all parties, as they all have an interest in disposing of cases. The group develops unwritten norms or rules of thumb to deal with cases that have no significant issues. The weak cases have already been screened out. No one has an interest in trying cases where there is little doubt as to the outcome. This dependence and cooperation is certainly contradictory to the ideal of the adversary system.

While judges retain the legal authority to make decisions, most decisions are made on a joint basis, as such shared decision making is based on a regularity of behavior and helps to diffuse responsibility among the court members. As the courtroom process becomes more predictable and cooperative, it becomes more efficient. Furthermore, decisions made on a joint basis help to protect the members of the workgroup and the integrity of the court.

New members of a courtroom workgroup soon learn the informal and formal requirements and norms of that particular court through the process of socialization. Through socialization, work group actors learn the shared norms. One set of norms revolve around the concept of the normal crime. As the majority of matters handled by courts are routine, they can be categorized by type and similarities into different types of normal crimes.

Courtroom actors who violate the norms or normative rules of the court can expect sanctions from the other members of the work group. Sanctions and behavior calling for sanctions disrupt the court's routine. Most actors follow the rules, which is generally rewarded, albeit slightly, with some leniency or other favorable outcome.

The degree to which the above five characteristics (*e.g.*, mutual interdependence, shared decision making, etc.) are found in individual courtrooms depends on a wide variety of variables. Among these are the views or support of the community and the turnover of individual work group members. The judge is usually the only relative constant. Maverick or hostile and aggressive attorneys change courtroom dynamics, but are likely to face sanctions and are rarely able to negotiate good deals for their clients.

While all courts face problems with delay, not all courts suffer from unnecessary delay. Furthermore, there is no consensus as to what constitutes unnecessary delay. Various commissions have come up with time periods ranging from six months to two years. However, the most commonly used benchmark is the American Bar Association's recommendation that all felony cases reach disposition within one year of filing.

The adage that "justice delayed is justice denied" is as old as the common law itself and reflects the historical philosophy that case delay undermines the values and integrity of the legal system. The three most often cited consequences of courtroom delay focus on defendants, society, and citizens. Historically, court delay was criticized for jeopardizing the defendant's right to a speedy trial, as provided in the Sixth Amendment. The federal government and most states have enacted speedy trial laws to protect defendants' rights to a speedy trial.

In a more contemporary view, delay has been viewed as hampering society's need for a speedy trial. In this view of a state's right to a speedy trial to protect the prosecution's case, many jurisdictions have enacted speedy trial laws. A third perspective views delay as it relates to the erosion of public confidence in the judicial system. In this view, delay not only causes the public to lose confidence in the system, but also forces victims, witnesses, and others to endure unnecessary and repeated trips to the courthouse. This may deter these individuals from getting involved in the future.

The varying views on delay have led to a difference in perceptions about the effects of delay. Some might view delay as encouraging defendants to enter plea bargains, while others may view delay as forcing prosecutors towards lenient plea bargains. While the National Center for State Courts has not found any evidence that case delay causes the deterioration of cases or lenient plea bargains, it has found that jail overcrowding and defendants skipping court appearances have led to case delay.

The law on the books approach to case delay focuses on resources and procedures. Examples would include adding judges, prosecutors, and other officials and streamlining court procedures. However, the National Center for State Courts has found that the relative size of caseloads, procedures, and emphasis on plea bargaining to be poor predictors of delay.

Speedy trial laws are probably the most prominent example of a law on the books panacea for court delay. While the U.S. Constitution and thirty-five state constitutions have guarantees for speedy trials, all states have some kind of speedy trial law. The Speedy Trial Act of 1974 (amended 1979) was enacted by Congress to specify the time standards for two primary stages of the federal court process. However, certain procedures, such as hearings on pretrial motions and the mental competency of the defendant are considered excludable time. While the federal speedy trial law was enacted to protect the interests of society, the state laws are generally oriented toward protecting defendants.

Because most speedy trial laws were enacted with little regard for the sources of court delay and provide few additional resources, speedy trial laws have, for the most part, proven ineffective. Furthermore, compliance with such laws has only been possible through the delaying of civil cases. However, federal speedy trial laws have proven to be quite effective. On average, in 1970 it took seven months for a criminal case to reach a disposition. In 1980, cases were disposed of in less than three months.

Law in action approaches to court delay focus on realistic approaches like coordination, improved scheduling, and cooperation. Such approaches have proven to be more effective than law on the books approaches. As just one person being late can delay an entire court proceeding, the focus on scheduling and improved administration has helped to get all the actors in the same place at the same time more often.

PRACTICE TEST BANK

Multiple Choice

1.   According to Neubauer, the most powerful member of the courtroom work group is the:
        _____.
        a.   defendant
        b.   judge
        c.   prosecutor
        d.   court administrator

2.   Most federal speedy trial laws are designed to protect _____.
        a.   defendants
        b.   the state
        c.   the interests of society
        d.   judicial integrity

3.   A prosecutor dropping a case for lack of sufficient evidence would be an example of
        what kind of discretion?
        a.   policy priorities
        b.   personal philosophies
        c.   rules of evidence
        d.   legal judgments

4.   Which of the following is not considered a court manager?
        a.   court clerk
        b.   chief judge
        c.   court administrator
        d.   sheriff

5.   Which of the following is a subcomponent of discretion?
        a.   caseload
        b.   court delay
        c.   policy priorities
        d.   routine administration

6.   The Speedy Trial Act of 1974 (amended 1979) allows for how many days from arrest to
        indictment in federal courts?
        a.   20
        b.   30
        c.   50
        d.   70

7. The federal Speedy Trial Act of 1974 (amended 1979) allows for how many days from indictment to trial?
    a. 20
    b. 30
    c. 50
    d. 70

8. Which of the following is another name sometimes used for a clerk of court?
    a. prothonotary
    b. calendar clerk
    c. registrar of record
    d. administrator of fact

9. Which of the following is not considered a routine duty of a court clerk?
    a. docketing cases
    b. overseeing jury selection
    c. writing opinions
    d. collection fees

10. Approximately how many people are arrested by police every year?
    a. 4 million
    b. 10 million
    c. 14 million
    d. 24 million

11. Approximately how many criminal offenders are arrested for felonies each year?
    a. 3 million
    b. 8 million
    c. 14 million
    d. 24 million

12. According to Neubauer, the most commonly advanced reason that criminal courts do not administer justice according to a "textbook image" is _____.
    a. court delay
    b. assembly-line justice
    c. discretion
    d. speedy trial laws

13. Which of the following is not characteristic of the courtroom work group?
    a. individual decision making
    b. mutual interdependence
    c. socialization
    d. rewards and sanctions

14. The average criminal case filed in federal courts in the 1970s took how many months to reach a disposition?
    a. three months
    b. five months
    c. seven months
    d. nine months

15. The average criminal case filed in federal courts in the 1980s was disposed of in how many months?
    a. three months
    b. five months
    c. seven months
    d. nine months

16. Which of the following is not a primary duty of a court administrator?
    a. prepare budgets
    b. troubleshooting
    c. summarizing caseload data
    d. docketing cases

17. Researchers agree that law-on-the-book approaches to court delays are _____.
    a. less effective than law in action approaches
    b. more effective than law in action approaches
    c. equally effective as law in action approaches
    d. not related to law in action approaches

18. In *Barker v. Wingo*, the Court held that _____.
    a. was violated by a five year delay
    b. is a relative, not an absolute, right
    c. is a right of the prosecution, but not the defense
    d. was an absolute constitutional mandate

19. The most common reason given for why criminal courts do not administer justice according to the textbook image is _____.
    a. discretion
    b. plea bargaining
    c. assembly-line justice
    d. court delay

20. Which of the following is not a finding of the National Center for State Courts?
    a. The level of court resources is not associated with delay.
    b. The size of caseload has little to do with delay.
    c. Plea bargaining made a huge difference in delay.
    d. Jail overcrowding and defendants skipping court may be related to delay.

True-False

1.   Federal speedy trial laws have proven quite effective.
       c.   true
       d.   false

2.   Plea bargaining became institutionalized as a part of American courts by the end of the nineteenth century.
       a.   true
       b.   false

3.   In large, urban courthouses, you will find many actors with specialized duties.
       a.   true
       b.   false

4.   Judges have traditionally competed with clerks of court for control over judicial administration.
       a.   true
       b.   false

5.   Discretion is used at very few stages in the criminal justice system.
       a.   true
       b.   false

6.   Courtroom dynamics strictly adhere to the adversarial model.
       a.   true
       b.   false

7.   Speedy trial laws are used in all fifty states.
       a.   true
       b.   false

8.   The National Center for State Courts has found caseload size and court procedures to have little effect on delay.
       a.   true
       b.   false

9.   A wooden podium separates the courthouse regulars from the occasional participants.
       a.   true
       b.   false

10.   The Second Amendment provides for the right to a speedy and public trial.
       a.   true
       b.   false

11. The bailiff is responsible for maintaining order in the courtroom.
   a.   true
   b.   false

12. Because criminal laws are so broad and general, they must be selectively enforced.
   a.   true
   b.   false

13. The Speedy Trial Act of 1974 (amended 1979) created extended time allowances for certain motions, known as includable time.
   a.   true
   b.   false

14. By the 1980s, every state had established a court administrator.
   a.   true
   b.   false

15. Entertainment and the media accurately portray the realities of courtroom justice.
   a.   true
   b.   false

Fill in the Blank

1. Most _____ speedy trial laws are designed to protect defendants.

2. In the thirteenth century, nobles forced King John to sign the _____ Carta.

3. The American _____ Association recommends that all felony cases reach disposition within one year of filing.

4. Today women account for anywhere from one third to one half of all _____ students.

5. Categorizing crimes and criminals on the basis of a typical manner in which they are committed is also known as normal _____.

6. Through _____ the courtroom work groups can make their common work site a predictable place to work.

7. Newcomers to a job learn the formal and informal rules of behavior through _____.

8. The shared decision making of the courtroom work group also helps to diffuse _____.

9. The imposition of sanctions can result in _____ being applied.

10. The position of the chief judge is really _____ among equals.

11. The _____Amendment provides for the right to a speedy and public trial.

12. The postponement or adjournment of proceedings in a case is generally referred to as a _____.

13. _____ attorneys often engage in hostile relations in court and are seldom able to negotiate effectively for good deals.

14. Generally presenting little dispute over fact or law, most case dispositions reflect _____ administration.

15. The court reporter or _____records a shorthand record of the court's proceedings.

Essay

1. List the three groups of people affected by court delay and explain how court delay affects each of the these groups

2. Describe and discuss the members and characteristics of the courtroom work group.

3. Explain the concept of assembly-line justice and give an example of how it might work in a court of law.

4. Explain discretion and its three major subcomponents. Give an example for each subcomponent.

5. Compare and contrast law on the books approaches to court delay versus law in action approaches to court delay.

CHAPTER 5 ANSWER KEYS

Multiple Choice

1—c	2—c	3—d	4—d	5—c
6—b	7—d	8—a	9—c	10—c
11—a	12—b	13—a	14—c	15—a
16—d	17—a	18—b	19—c	20—c

True-False

1—a	2—a	3—a	4—a	5—b
6—b	7—a	8—a	9—b	10—b
11—a	12—a	13—c	14—a	15—b

Fill in the blank

1—state	2—Magna	3—Bar	4—law
5—crimes	6—cooperation	7—socialization	8—responsibility
9—counter-sanction	10—first	11—Sixth	12—delay
13—Maverick	14—routine	15—stenographer	

Chapter 6
PROSECUTORS

LEARNING OBJECTIVES

After reading this chapter, students should understand the

- role of prosecutors in the criminal justice system.
- nature of prosecution in the federal courts.
- nature of prosecution in the state courts.
- activities central to prosecutor's office work.
- relationship between prosecutors and the courtroom work group.
- expanding authority of prosecutors.

CHAPTER OUTLINE

I.   **Role of the Prosecutor**
    A.   Broad Discretion
    B.   Decentralization

II.   **Prosecution in Federal Courts**
    A.   Solicitor General
    B.   Criminal Division of the Justice Department
    C.   U.S. Attorneys

III. **Prosecution in State Courts**
    A.   State Attorney General
        1.   State's chief legal and law enforcement officer
        2.   Growing emphasis on civil responsibilities
    B.   Chief Prosecutors
        1.   Chief law enforcement officer of their jurisdiction
        2.   Prosecutors are generally elected officials
    C.   Local Prosecutor
        1.   Represents the government in preliminary stages of felony cases
        2.   Process minor criminal offenses in lower courts

IV.   **The Prosecutor's Office at Work**
    A.   Assistant District Attorneys
        1.   High turnover rate due to law salary and heavy caseloads
    B.   Learning the Job
        1.   Evaluated by how quickly and efficiently they dispose of cases
    C.   Promotions and Office Structure
    D.   Supervision
    E.   Attempts at Greater Supervision

V.   Prosecutorial Ethics
    A.   Disclosure of information
    B.   Conflict of interests

VI.   Prosecutors and Courtroom Work Groups
    A.   The prosecutor is the most important member of the work group.
        1.   Prosecutors set the agenda and control cases through discretion
    B.   Conflicting Goals and Contrasting Work Groups
    C.   Political Styles and Contrasting Work Groups
        1.   Office conservator
        2.   Courthouse insurgents
        3.   Policy reformers

VII. The Expanding Domain of the Prosecutor
    A.   Improving Police-Prosecutor Relationships
        1.   Inadequate reports
        2.   Thoroughness of police investigations
    B.   Community Prosecution

VIII. Conclusion

KEY TERMS

local prosecutors - General term for lawyers who represent local governments (cities and counties, for example) in the lower courts; often called *city attorneys* or *solicitors*. (129)

officer of the court - Lawyers are officers of the court and, as such, must obey court rules, be truthful in court, and generally serve the needs of justice. (122)

prosecutor - A public official who represents the state in a criminal action. (129)

solicitor general - Third-ranking official in the U.S. Department of Justice who conducts and supervises government litigation before the Supreme Court. (126)

state attorney general - The chief legal officer of a state, representing that state in civil and, under certain circumstances, criminal cases. (127)

U.S. attorney general - Head of the Department of Justice; nominated by the president and confirmed by the Senate. (125)

U.S. attorneys - Officials responsible for the prosecution of crimes that violate the laws of the United States; appointed by the president and assigned to a U.S. district court. (126)

CHAPTER SUMMARY

Prosecutors are generally the most powerful officials in criminal courts and in the courtroom work group. Due to their unique positions, prosecutors work with all actors of the criminal justice system and have broad discretion and judicial independence. Supreme Court Justice Robert Jackson once remarked that "The prosecutor has more control over life, liberty, and reputation than any other person in America." American prosecutors' offices are characterized by autonomy and decentralization, having more power, independence, and discretion than any of their counterparts in other nations.

Federal prosecution falls under the auspices of the U.S. Department of Justice. The Attorney General heads this cabinet agency. The U.S. Attorney General is nominated by the President and confirmed by the Senate, a member of the President's cabinet, and the nation's chief law enforcement officer. The U.S. Attorney General also supervises U.S. attorneys.

U.S. Attorneys prosecute violations of federal law. There are 93 U.S. Attorneys, generally one for each district; the one exception is that one attorney serves Guam and the Northern Mariana Islands. U.S. Attorneys are also appointed by the President and confirmed by the Senate. They serve at the will of the president and are the chief law enforcement officers for their respective districts.

The U.S. Solicitor General serves a unique role in representing the U.S. government's interests in and before the Supreme Court. Because of their influence, this office is commonly referred to as the "Tenth Justice." The Solicitor General's office argues all government cases before the Supreme Court. Generally, all government agencies must receive authorization from the Solicitor General to appeal an adverse lower court ruling to the Supreme Court. As the office only requests review of cases which have a high degree of policy significance and in which the government has a reasonable argument, the solicitor general has a high rate of success in petitioning the Supreme Court and winning cases argued on their merits.

The state attorney general is the state's chief legal officer. However, with the majority of states having highly decentralized prosecutors' offices, the state attorney general has limited authority over criminal matters. State attorney generals have, however, become highly visible and active in civil matters such as consumer complaints, child support and product liability cases.

Chief prosecutors, also known as district attorneys, prosecuting attorneys, or county attorneys, are the chief law enforcement officers of their jurisdictions. Around 95% of chief prosecutors are locally elected officials and typically serve four-year terms.

Local prosecutors (*e.g.*, city and county attorneys) are local officials responsible for prosecuting minor criminal offenses and misdemeanors. They also sometimes represent the state in the preliminary stages of felony cases.

Assistant district attorneys are generally hired fresh out of law school or after a short time in private practice. Assistants have a high turnover rate due to heavy caseloads and relatively low salaries. While training has traditionally been on the job, prosecutors' offices have started to train assistant district attorneys more systematically.

Larger cities use the horizontal form of prosecution in which prosecutors are assigned to specific functions (*e.g.*, doing only grand jury or only preliminary hearings). Smaller jurisdictions use vertical prosecution in which a prosecutor is assigned to a case from intake to appeal.

Traditionally centered on autonomy, prosecutors' offices are moving to more controlling bureaucratic methods for greater control and supervision of prosecutors within their office. Assistants have more rules and regulations and thus less discretion.

While the most powerful member of the courtroom work group, prosecutors are still influenced by the judge and defense attorneys, as they can also be sanctioned for acting outside of the work group norms. Thus, prosecutors must still work within the constraints of the courtroom work group.

As political officers, prosecutors may adopt one of three political styles: office conservator (protect status quo), courthouse insurgent (aggressive reformer), or policy reformer (gradual reformer). Flemming found that differences in political styles cross party lines and may change over time.

While police and prosecutors have differing duties and perspectives within the criminal justice system, they share close ties in disposing of cases. Accordingly, prosecutors have increasingly tried programs and procedures to increase police-prosecutor coordination and communication. However, little research has been done on the effectiveness of these programs.

Community prosecution is a relatively new proactive approach adopted by prosecutors to address community problems. Such problem-oriented approaches have three elements in common: crime prevention is recognized as a legitimate goal, the most effective results are obtained within small, manageable geographic areas, and change is more likely to occur through cooperation with communities.

PRACTICE TEST BANK

Multiple Choice

1. Which of the following justices once remarked, "The prosecutor has more control over life, liberty, and reputation than any other person in America?"
   a. Robert Jackson
   b. William Howard Taft
   c. John Jay
   d. Earl Warren

2. The office of the prosecutor is part of which branch of government?
   a. executive
   b. judicial
   c. legislative
   d. administrative

3. Which of the following is billed as the world's largest law firm?
   a. Federal Bureau of Investigation
   b. State Department
   c. Department of Justice
   d. U.S. Attorney's Office

4. What is the current number of U.S. attorneys?
   a. 23
   b. 63
   c. 93
   d. 103

5. Within the criminal justice system, who is in the best position to provide coordination?
   a. judges
   b. police chiefs
   c. probation officers
   d. prosecutors

6. In which case did the Supreme Court say that "while a prosecutor may strike hard blows, he is not at liberty to strike foul ones?"
   a. Berger v. U.S.
   b. Burns v. Reed
   c. Miranda v. Arizona
   d. Terry v. Ohio

7. All federal agencies must receive permission from whom before appealing an adverse lower court ruling to the Supreme Court?
   a. U.S. solicitor general
   b. U.S. attorneys
   c. Supreme Court chief justice
   d. U.S. attorney general

8. Which of the following is not a common element of community prosecution?
   a. the recognition that crime prevention is a legitimate prosecutorial concern
   b. the most effective results are obtained with small, manageable geographic areas
   c. the most effective results are obtained by focusing on individual arrests
   d. change is more likely to occur through cooperative efforts

9. U.S. attorneys serve _____.
   a. life terms
   b. four year terms
   c. ten year terms
   d. at the pleasure of the president

10. U.S. attorneys are _____.
    a. chosen in district elections
    b. appointed by the attorney general
    c. nominated by the president and confirmed by the Senate
    d. appointed by the solicitor general

11. Small prosecutor offices generally employ what type of prosecution?
    a. horizontal
    b. perpendicular
    c. parallel
    d. vertical

12. Large prosecutor offices generally employ what type of prosecution?
    a. horizontal
    b. perpendicular
    c. parallel
    d. vertical

13. There are approximately how many chief prosecutors nationwide?
    a. 1300
    b. 2300
    c. 4300
    d. 9300

14. Which of the following is not considered responsible for processing cases in lower courts?
    a. solicitors
    b. city attorneys
    c. district attorneys
    d. local prosecutors

15. Research concerning programs to improve police-prosecutor relationships has _____ .
    a. found such programs to be quite effective
    b. found such programs to be ineffective
    c. been inconclusive
    d. been virtually nonexistent

16. What is the estimated total number of federal, state, county, municipal, and township prosecution agencies in the nation?
    a. 800
    b. 2300
    c. 8000
    d. 18000

17. How many staff attorneys commonly assist the solicitor general?
    a. 9
    b. 12
    c. 23
    d. 35

18. The solicitor general's office generally requests Supreme Court review only in cases with a high degree of significance and _____ .
    a. in which the government is a party
    b. in which the government has a reasonable legal argument
    c. which involves the U.S. Constitution
    d. which involves federal employees

19. U.S. attorneys fall under the supervision of _____ .
    a. the solicitor general
    b. the vice president
    c. the attorney general
    d. their constituents

20. One U.S. attorney covers both _____ .
    a. Puerto Rico and the Virgin Islands
    b. Puerto Rico and Guam
    c. Guam and the Northern Mariana Islands
    d. The Virgin Islands and the Northern Mariana Islands

True-False

1. Prosecution in the United States is highly decentralized.
   a. true
   b. false

2. The Justice Department quadrupled in size from 1981 to 1993.
   a. true
   b. false

3. The solicitor general has a low rate of success in petitioning the Supreme Court and in winning cases argued on their merits.
   a. true
   b. false

4. With one exception, there are two U.S. attorneys assigned to each district.
   a. true
   b. false

5. Compared to their counterparts, American prosecutors have much less independence and discretionary power.
   a. true
   b. false

6. The county judge is the chief law enforcement officer of the community.
   a. true
   b. false

7. The majority of prosecutors are elected and not appointed.
   a. true
   b. false

8. Turnover rates among assistant district attorneys is relatively high.
   a. true
   b. false

9. Specialization has been decreasing among prosecutors' offices, especially in larger jurisdictions.
   a. true
   b. false

10. Many prosecutor offices have been moving away from autonomy to more controlling bureaucratic management.
    a. true
    b. false

11.   Judges commonly control the flow of information about cases.
        a.   true
        b.   false

12.   Community prosecution is considered a problem-oriented approach.
        a.   true
        b.   false

13.   In the courtroom environment, not losing a case is more important than winning.
        a.   true
        b.   false

14.   State attorney generals usually have great authority over local criminal procedures.
        a.   true
        b.   false

15.   Politics have little effect on prosecutorial selection.
        a.   true
        b.   false

Fill in the Blank

1.   The U.S. _____ general is often referred to as the Tenth Justice.

2.   The state _____ general is the state's chief legal officer and law enforcement official.

3.   The traditional form of prosecutorial management is centered on _____.

4.   Under the adversarial model of justice, prosecutors view all cases as _____ and often overcharge.

5.   Under the _____ of justice model, prosecutors only concentrate on serious offenses and follow strict standards when charging.

6.   Prosecutors who accept the status quo, adopt the office _____ style

7.   Courthouse _____ are dissatisfied with the status quo and will fight to change it.

8.   Policy _____ are dissatisfied with the status quo, but are cautious in their approaches to change it.

9.   _____ prosecution stresses a proactive approach.

10.   U.S. attorneys are responsible for the prosecution of crimes violating _____ laws.

11. In _____ prosecution, separate prosecutors are assigned to specific court functions.

12. In _____ prosecution, a prosecutor is assigned a case from intake to appeal.

13. Approximately 95 percent of chief prosecutors are elected _____.

14. The chief prosecutor has numerous opportunities for political _____.

15. The office of prosecutor is part of the _____ branch of government.

Essay

1. Describe and discuss the structure, titles, and duties of those involved in federal prosecution from trial to U.S. Supreme Court argument.

2. Compare and contrast horizontal and vertical organization in prosecutors' officers.

3. Explain and discuss the differences between the adversarial and administrative models of justice.

4. List the pros and cons of prosecutorial decentralization.

5. Is the prosecutor the most influential and powerful actor of the courtroom work group? Defend your answer.

CHAPTER 6 ANSWER KEYS

Multiple Choice

1—a	2—a	3—c	4—c	5—d
6—a	7—a	8—c	9—d	10—c
11—d	12—a	13—b	14—c	15—d
16—c	17—c	18—b	19—c	20—c

True-False

1—T	2—T	3—F	4—F	5—F
6—F	7—T	8—T	9—F	10—T
11—F	12—T	13—T	14—F	15—F

Fill in the blank

1—solicitor	2—attorney	3—autonomy	4—serious
5—administration	6—conservator	7—insurgents	8—reformers
9—community	10—federal	11—horizontal	12—vertical
13—locally	14—patronage	15—executive	

Chapter 7
DEFENSE ATTORNEYS

LEARNING OBJECTIVES

After reading this chapter, students should understand the

- Sixth Amendment's right to counsel.
- ineffective assistance of counsel and self-representation.
- role of the defense attorney's relationship to the courtroom work group.
- diversity and stratification of the legal profession.
- nature of providing indigents with attorneys.
- role of the public defender in the criminal justice system.
- the nature of interactions between defense attorneys and their clients.

CHAPTER OUTLINE

I. **The Right to Counsel**
    A. *Gideon v. Wainwright*—6th Amendment indigent right to counsel
    B. *In re Gault*—extended *Gideon* to juveniles
    C. Nonfelony Criminal Prosecutions
        1. *Argersinger v. Hamlin*—limits indigent right to counsel only in cases which lead to imprisonment
    D. Stages of the Criminal Process
    E. Ineffective Assistance of Counsel
        1. *Strickland v. Washington*—applies objective reasonableness standard to effective counsel
    F. Self-Representation
        1. *Faretta v. California*—defendant need not have the skills and experience of a lawyer for self-representation

II. **Defense Attorneys and Courtroom Work Groups**
    A. How defense attorneys act and plan their defense is directly related to their relationship with other members of the courtroom work group
    B. Defense attorneys are the least powerful members of the courtroom work group.
    C. Rewards and Sanctions
    D. Variations in Cooperation
    E. An Assessment
        1. Defense attorneys who handle few criminal cases
        2. Defense attorneys who practice criminal law and maintain hostile relationships with prosecutors' offices (gamblers)
        3. Studies show mixed results on the effectiveness of private vs. public defense attorneys

III. The Criminal Bar

  A. Diversity and Stratification of the Legal Corporate or organizational
    1. Personal business
    2. The majority of attorneys who appear in criminal court are from the personal client sector.
  B. Environment of Practice
    1. Low status and reputation
    2. Difficulty in securing clients
    3. Low fees

IV. Providing Indigents with Attorneys

  A. Assigned Counsel
    1. Involves appointment from a list of available private attorneys
  B. Contract Systems
    1. Involves bidding by private attorneys to represent all indigent defendants for a fixed payment
  C. Public Defenders
    1. Salaried public officials to represent indigent defendants
    2. Today represents 70% of all defendants nationwide
  D. Assessing the Merits of Public Defenders

V. Lawyers and Clients

  A. Privileged communications
  B. Lawyers View Their Clients
    1. Refusal to cooperate, deception, and dishonesty pose serious problems for defense attorneys
    2. Private attorneys find their advice accepted more often than court appointed lawyers.
  C. Defendants View Their Lawyers
    1. Clients skeptical of lawyer skills

VI. Defense Attorney Ethics

  A. Defending unpopular clients
  B. Confidentiality issues

VII. Conclusion

KEY TERMS

assigned counsel system - Arrangement that provides attorneys for persons who are accused of crimes and are unable to hire their own lawyers. The judge assigns a member of the bar to provide counsel to a particular defendant. (154)

contract system - Method of providing counsel for indigents under which the government contracts with a law firm to represent all indigents for the year in return for a set fee. (154)

indigents - Defendants who are too poor to pay a lawyer and therefore are entitled to a lawyer for free. (153)

privileged communication - A recognized right to keep certain communications confidential or private. (157)

public defender - An attorney employed by the government to represent indigent defendants. (154)

pro se - Acting as one's own attorney in court. Representing oneself. (148)

right to counsel - Right of the accused to the services of a lawyer paid for by the government, established by the Sixth Amendment and extended by the Warren Court (*Gideon v. Wainwright*) to indigent defendants in felony cases. (144)

CHAPTER SUMMARY

In 1963, *Gideon v. Wainwright* emphasized the importance of lawyers for defense by holding that based on the Sixth Amendment right to counsel, indigent defendants charged with a felony are entitled to a lawyer paid for by the government. The Court extended the right to counsel to juveniles in the *In re Gault* case of 1967. *Argersinger v. Hamlin* held that the right to counsel does not extend to those accused of only minor violations. *Scott v. Illinois* held that legal counsel is guaranteed only in cases that actually lead to imprisonment. The Court ruled in *Ross v. Moffitt* that indigents have no right to counsel in discretionary appeals and appeals to the Supreme Court. One consequence of this decision is that defendants sentenced to death must rely on voluntary counsel to pursue postconviction remedies. However, some state supreme courts have mandated more extensive and protective rights than the Supreme Court.

The Court ruled in *McMann v. Richardson* that the effective assistance of counsel is also guaranteed by the Sixth Amendment and created an "objective standard of reasonableness" criterion for determining the ineffectiveness of counsel. Basically, appellate courts must reverse only if the proceedings were fundamentally unfair and the outcome would have been different if counsel had not been ineffective. As the burden of proof lies heavily on the claimant, there are relatively few reversals. In *Faretta v. California*, the Court ruled that defendants who wish to represent themselves must show the judge that they have the ability to conduct the trial, thus supporting a right to self-representation. Nevertheless, self-representation is rare.

As officers of the court, defense attorneys are bound to fulfill their responsibilities within the framework of established legal ethics. How defense attorneys proceed with a client's case also depends on their relationship with the courtroom work group. Defense attorneys who maintain a cooperative stance with the work group often reap the benefits for both themselves and their clients. However, hostile defense attorneys can be sanctioned by other members of the work group. While sanctions are rarely used, they can have dire effects.

Defense attorneys are the least powerful members of the courtroom work group and as such are forced to take a reactive posture. Skolnick classifies defense attorneys into three categories. The first is made up of attorneys who handle few criminal cases and whose inexperience makes them unpredictable and often causes administrative problems. The second category is made up of active criminal attorneys who maintain hostile relationships with the prosecutor's office, known as "gamblers." The third category is made up of public defenders and private attorneys who represent large numbers of defendants and work within the system. Research studying the effectiveness of public defenders versus private attorneys has found mixed results.

There are basically two types of lawyers based on clientele, lawyers who represent large organizations (known as the corporate client sector), and those who represent individuals, known as the personal client sector. The personal client sector is divided into personal business and personal plight. The majority of attorneys who appear in criminal court come from the personal client sector. Corporations rarely find themselves in criminal court.

Low status, difficulty in securing clients, and low fees are three factors that affect the availability of lawyers to represent criminal defendants. The criminal lawyer's most important commodity in securing clients is his or her reputation. Some attorneys rely on police officers, bail agents, and court clerks to give their names to defendants who need counsel. Lawyer's fees in criminal cases are generally flat fees and the three most important considerations in setting fees are the seriousness of the offense, the amount of time necessary for the case, and the client's ability to pay.

Around 75% of state prison inmates had a court-appointed lawyer to represent them for the offense for which they were serving time. In urban areas, 80% of felony defendants are indigent. In most jurisdictions, local governments foot the bill for providing criminal defense to the poor. In the U.S., there are three primary methods for assigning counsel to the indigent: assigned counsel, contract systems, and public defender systems. Assigned counsel is used in half of all U.S. counties but represents less than one third of the nation's population. It predominates in small counties with less than 50,000 residents, which lack the sufficient volume of cases to support the costs of a public defender system. The primary advantage of contract systems is that they limit government costs for indigent defense. However, the supreme courts of several states have found legal defects in contract systems. The public defender system is the oldest and most popular system, representing approximately 70% of all indigents nationwide. This system was started in Los Angeles County in 1914. Studies comparing assigned counsel to public offenders have found little difference.

In civil litigation, the relationship between lawyer and client is often characterized by trust and full disclosure. In criminal cases, the relationship is more often characterized by distrust and hostility. Defense attorneys also cite refusal to cooperate, deception, and dishonesty as problems in dealing with clients. Interestingly, private attorneys find their advice accepted more readily than court-appointed lawyers do. As most defender's offices are organized on a zone basis, part of the explanation for the breakdown of the client-public offender relationship involves the absence of one-to-one contact. Regardless of validity, defendant's lack of trust and confidence in their lawyers is a major force shaping the dynamics of courthouse justice.

PRACTICE TEST BANK

Multiple Choice

1. In the case *Gideon v. Wainwright* (1963), the Supreme Court decided that _____.
    a   defendants are entitled to a fast and speedy trial
    b.   all indigent defendants are entitled to court appointed counsel in felony trails
    c.   only those who can afford an attorney may have one
    d.   it is up to the individual state whether a person is assigned an attorney or not

2. Which of the following Supreme Court cases included the right to counsel for juveniles?
    a.   *Scott v. Illinois*
    b.   *Mempa v. Rhay*
    c.   *In re Gault*
    d.   *McKaskle v. Wiggins*

3. Self representation is limited to those who _____.
    a.   have a law degree
    b.   cannot afford an attorney
    c.   anyone who wants to represent themselves
    d.   can show the trial judge that they have an ability to conduct the trial

4. In discretionary appeals and appeals to the Supreme Court, indigent defendants have no right to court-appointed counsel according to what case?
    a.   *McMann v. Richardson*
    b.   *Faretta v. California*
    c.   *Ross v. Moffitt*
    d.   *Brewer v. Williams*

5. One advantage to the public defender system is that _____.
    a.   it provides more experienced, competent counsel
    b.   an attorney is appointed by a judge
    a.   the attorney is paid on a case by case basis
    b.   they are private for-profit organizations only

6. Contract systems are most often found in counties with populations of less than _____.
    a.   30,000
    b.   65,000
    c.   45,000
    d.   50,000

7. One's right to counsel does not extend to those who are accused of minor violations (misdemeanor or ordinance violations) according to which Supreme Court case?
   a. *Gideon v. Wainwright*
   b. *U. S. v. Wade*
   c. *Argersinger v. Hamlin*
   d. *Roe v. Flores Ortega*

8. Important considerations in setting fees include _____.
   a. seriousness of the offense, amount of time to deal with the case, and client's ability to pay
   b. who the client is and how much they can pay
   c. who will pay the bill, how big is the case, and how much time will be involved
   d. type of offense, is the person indigent or not, and what could the possible outcome be

9. Which type of lawyer has major concerns with collecting and receiving fees?
   a. corporate lawyers
   b. public defenders
   c. criminal lawyers
   d. solo practitioners

10. Who ultimately decides whether or not a defendant pleas guilty or goes to trial?
    a. Prosecutor
    b. Defendant
    c. Judge
    d. Defense attorney

11. Defense attorneys known as "gamblers" _____.
    a. are inexperienced
    b. represent large numbers of clients and work with prosecutors
    c. maintain a hostile relationship with the prosecutor's office
    d. are unpredictable and cause administrative problems

12. Most lawyers avoid representing criminal defendants because _____.
    a. it produces few chances of victory
    b. of high fees
    c. of high status
    d. of letting the guilty go free

13. Critics of the assigned counsel system contend that _____.
    a. there is no guarantee that the lawyer chosen will be qualified to handle criminal law
    b. public defenders should be hired to represent indigents
    c. the appointed lawyers are often unwilling to serve as assigned counsel
    d. attorneys are inadequately compensated for their time

14.   Clients are more likely to accept advice from private attorneys than court appointed lawyers because _____.
        a.   the client has the choice in who he or she hires to represent them
        b.   court appointed lawyers are less knowledgeable
        c.   private attorneys are more favorable among judges
        d.   court appointed lawyers are more accountable to the community

15.   _____ depend on the defense attorney to pressure defendants to plead guilty.
        a.   The community and victims
        b.   Judges and prosecutors
        c.   Victims and their families
        d.   Prosecutors and the community

16.   Public defenders are usually assigned _____.
        a.   to a circuit of judges
        b.   to three or four courtrooms
        c.   to two or three judges
        d.   permanently to a single courtroom and work everyday with the same judge

17.   The Courts ruling in *Gideon v. Wainwright* was limited to _____.
        a.   federal capital cases
        b.   state felony prosecutions
        c.   state misdemeanor cases
        d.   all criminal cases, both felony and misdemeanor

18.   What is the average percentage of state prison inmates who have a court-appointed lawyer to represent them for the offense for which they are serving?
        a.   10%
        b.   25%
        c.   50%
        d.   75%

19.   Which method of providing legal representation for the indigent is the most popular in large cities?
        a.   assigned counsel
        b.   contract
        c.   public defender
        d.   *pro bono*

20.   The National Advisory Commission on Criminal Justice Standards and Goals recommends that a maximum effective felony caseload per attorney per year is how many cases?
        a.   50
        b.   100
        c.   150
        d.   200

True-False

1. The 6th Amendment provides the right to counsel in "all criminal prosecutions."
    a. true
    b. false

2. Defendants whose cases do not lead to imprisonment have the right to counsel.
    a. true
    b. false

3. Self- representation rarely occurs in criminal trials.
    a. true
    b. false

4. Unlike prosecutors, defense attorneys are not considered as officers of the court.
    a. true
    b. false

5. Law is a diverse profession based partially on the law school attended and the place of work.
    a. true
    b. false

6. Assigned counsel systems involve the appointment by the court of private attorneys from a list of available attorneys.
    a. true
    b. false

7. Defendants do not have a Sixth Amendment right to the assistance of counsel once any adversary proceedings have begun.
    a. true
    b. false

8. Contract systems involve bidding by private attorneys to represent all criminal defendants found indigent during the term of the contract.
    a. true
    b. false

9. In most criminal cases a lawyer's fee is generally a flat rate paid in advance.
    a. true
    b. false

10. Defense attorneys may rely on police officers, bail agents/bondsmen, or court clerks to give their names to prospective clients.
    a. true
    b. false

11. Defense attorneys are the most powerful members of the courtroom work group.
    a. true
    a. false

12. The bulk of the attorneys who appear in criminal court are drawn from the personal client sector.
    a. true
    b. false

13. The criminal lawyer's most important commodity in securing clients is his or her reputation.
    a. true
    b. false

14. Despite a legal presumption of innocence, once defendants are arrested, the public assumes they are guilty.
    a. true
    b. false

15. Public defenders find their advice accepted more readily than private attorneys do.
    a. true
    b. false

Fill in the Blank

1. *Gideon v.* _____ established the right to counsel for all indigent defendants.

2. Those who choose not to obtain a lawyer, but decide to go to court on their own are practicing self-_____.

3. Defendants who are too poor to pay a lawyer and are entitled to a lawyer for free are considered _____.

4. The three primary methods of providing legal representation in the U. S. are assigned _____, contract systems, and public defenders.

5. The Supreme Court held that the Mohave County contract system, which assigned defense representation of the indigent to the _____ bidder, violated the Fifth and Sixth Amendments.

6. _____ percent of felony defendants are too poor to hire their own lawyer.

7. Statements made by a client to his or her attorney are considered _____ communications.

8. Defense attorneys are the _____ powerful members of the courtroom work group.

9. The Latin term _____ *se* means "in his or her own behalf."

10. As an officer of the _____, attorneys must work within the confines established by legal ethics.

11. Part of the reason for the breakdown of trust between the client and public _____ is the lack of one-to-one contact.

12. Defense attorneys who maintain a _____ stance towards the other members of the courtroom work group can expect to reap some rewards.

13. The _____ counsel system is used in over half of all U.S. counties, but serves less than one third of the nation's population.

14. The primary advantage of _____ systems is that they limit the costs governments must pay for indigent defense.

15. In most states, the _____ government pays for indigent defense.

Essay

1. List and describe the three primary methods for assigning counsel for indigent defendants in the U.S.

2. List three Supreme Court cases dealing with the right to counsel and explain their significance.

3. Discuss the relationship between defense attorneys and the courtroom work group and how it affects the outcome and proceedings for their defendants.

4. What have been the findings of research studying the difference between privately retained attorneys and public defenders?

5. Discuss some of the problems that defense attorneys have with defending criminal clients.

CHAPTER 7 ANSWER KEYS

Multiple Choice

1—b	2—c	3—d	4—c	5—a
6—d	7—c	8—a	9—c	10—b
11—c	12—a	13—a	14—a	15—b
16—d	17—b	18—d	19—c	20—c

True-False

1—F	2—F	3—T	4—F	5—T
6—T	7—F	8—T	9—T	10—T
11—F	12—T	13—T	14—T	15—F

Fill in the blank

1—*Wainwright*	2—representation	3—indigents	4—counsel
5—lowest	6—80	7—privileged	8—least
9—pro	10—court	11—defender	12—cooperative
13—assigned	14—contract	15—local	

Chapter 8
JUDGES

LEARNING OBJECTIVES

After reading this chapter, students should understand the

- functions of being a judge in the criminal justice system.
- role of judges within the courtroom work group.
- various selection processes used for judges.
- consequences of methods used to select judges.
- nature of diversity and the judiciary.
- assessment processes of judicial performance.
- various methods used to retain and remove judges from the legal system.

CHAPTER OUTLINE

I.   **The Position of the Judge**
    A.   Powers of the Judge
    B.   Benefits
        1.   Judges have been afforded a high level of prestige and respect
    C.   Frustrations of the Job
        1.   Heavy caseloads and administrative problems

II.   **Judges within the Courtroom Work Group**
    A.   Sanctions can be applied against judges who violate the norms of the work group by prosecutors and defense attorneys.
    B.   Judges are the most prestigious members of the work group.

III.   **Varying Roads to a Judgeship**
    A.   Executive appointment
        1.   Article III judges are appointed by the president.
        2.   Only a few states use outright gubernatorial appointment.
    B.   Election of Judges
        1.   More than half of the states select judges through popular judicial elections.
        2.   Politics play a role in both partisan and nonpartisan elections.
    C.   Merit Selection
        1.   Missouri Bar Plan (hybrid system)
            a.   Judicial nominating commission of laypersons and lawyers
            b.   The state's chief executive (governor) makes the final selection
            c.   Retention elections are held

IV.   **Consequences of Judicial Selection**
    A.   Which system is Best?
        1.   Elective systems tend to elect those who have held prior political office
        2.   Merit systems also tend to elect former district attorneys as judges

B.   Similarities in Judges' Backgrounds
  1.   Male
  2.   White
  3.   Protestant
  4.   Upper middle class background
  5.   Above average education

C.   Diversity and the Judiciary
  1.   The under-representation of blacks on the bench is a partial reflection of the small number of blacks practicing law
  2.   The under-representation of blacks on the bench is also a product of judicial selection
  3.   Women make up approximately 25% of lawyers practicing criminal law
  4.   Today 21% of state appellate court judges are women

V.   Judging the Judges

A.   Judicial Independence
  1.   Protections against unpopular rulings are the hallmark of judicial independence

B.   Judicial Misconduct
  1.   Corruption
  2.   Scandal
  3.   Impairment—many states have enacted voluntary retirement ages for judges

C.   State Judicial Conduct Commissions
  1.   Commissions investigate claims and complaints
  2.   Commissions may admonish, censure, or demand retirement or removal
  3.   State supreme courts retain the final power to discipline errant judges

D.   Federal Conduct and Disability Act
  1.   In 1980, Congress passed the Judicial Councils Reform and Judicial Conduct and Disability Act
  2.   Judicial councils of each U.S. Court of Appeals hear complaints and investigate
  3.   Serious findings are reported to the Judicial Conference, which may recommend action by the U.S. House of Representatives
  4.   Impeachment is used in the most serious cases

VI.   Judicial Ethics

  1.   Lack of understanding reflects misconduct accusations
  2.   Public criticism based on unpopular decisions

VII.   Conclusion

KEY TERMS

American Bar Association (ABA) - The largest voluntary organization of lawyers in the United States. (172)

chambers - The private office of a judge. (166)

gubernatorial appointment - Method of judicial selection in which the governor appoints a person to a judicial vacancy without an election. (172)

impeachment - Official accusation against a public official brought by a legislative body seeking his or her removal. (180)

judicial conduct commission - An official body whose function is to investigate allegations of misconduct by judges. (180)

judicial election - Method of judicial selection in which the voters choose judicial candidates in a partisan or nonpartisan election. (172)

judicial independence - Normative value that stresses a judge should be free from outside pressure in making a decision. (177)

Missouri Bar Plan - The name given to a method of judicial selection combining merit selection and popular control in retention elections. (173)

removal - To dismiss a person from holding office. (180)

CHAPTER SUMMARY

To most Americans, the judge is the symbol of justice. Of all the actors in the criminal justice system, the public holds the judge most responsible for ensuring that the system operates fairly and impartially.

The formal powers of judges are evident throughout the criminal justice system. Judges preside over the decisions that affect defendants at all stages of the justice system. Judges also decide key cases that affect policy and the actions of criminal justice officials. Judges enjoy high levels of prestige and respect. Judges are among the highest paid in the criminal justice system and enjoy considerable opportunity for patronage. However, many judges also encounter frustration with heavy caseloads and corresponding administrative problems. Furthermore, judges are dependent on many other players in the courtroom, in essence limiting their power and effectiveness.

As the most prestigious members of the courtroom work group, judges also retain the formal legal powers of their office, but informally share them with other members of the work group. The relationship of the courtroom work group is characterized by cooperation enforced by sanctions available to all members. In most instances, the judge knows less about the case than the attorneys.

Which lawyers become judges is selected by formal selection methods and informal procedures. Half of all trial judges initially received their position through some sort of interim or vacancy position. There are three major methods used in judicial selection: executive appointment, elections, and merit selection.

The most common example of executive appointment is the appointment of Article III judges by the president with consent of the Senate. Gubernatorial appointments are another example of executive appointment.

More than half of all states select judges through popular judicial elections. Whether partisan or nonpartisan elections are used, politics still play a role in elections. Incumbent judges rarely loose elections.

Merit selection is also referred to as the Missouri Bar Plan because Missouri was the first state to adopt this hybrid form of selection in 1940. Merit selection begins with a committee of laypersons and lawyers who compose a list of qualified nominees. The state's chief executive makes the final selection from the list of qualified candidates. After a short time in office, a retention election is held in which the public votes whether or not to keep the newly appointed judge in office. Proponents claim that merit selection puts better-qualified judges on the bench. Merit selection is growing in popularity and contrary to its proponents, merit selection does not take the politics out of judicial selection, but merely alters it.

There is no systematic evidence that one selection system produces better judges than another selection system. However, there is evidence that state supreme court justices selected by partisan elections react to public opinions, whereas those appointed by governors are more free of constraint.

Traditionally, judges have been white, Protestant, males from upper middle class families with above average educations. Judges in general are also very likely to have held public office. The numbers of women and minorities on the bench is growing. Most research finds very little difference between the decisions of judges of different race and gender.

While judicial independence is a key to the effectiveness of the American judiciary, procedures must be in place to maintain the integrity of and the public's confidence in the judiciary through the disciplining and removal of errant judges. In 1960, California became the first state to adopt a modern and practical system for disciplining judges in the form of a judicial conduct commission. Such commissions are found in very state and investigate and act on claims of misconduct. Actions may include admonishment, censure, or the demand of retirement or removal. Final power to discipline judges falls to the state supreme courts. In 1980, Congress passed the Judicial Councils Reform and Judicial Conduct and Disability Act, which lays out procedures for handling complaints. Complaints are initially heard by the judicial councils of the U.S. Courts of Appeals. Serious cases are reported to the Judicial Conference, which may recommend that the U.S. House of Representatives begin impeachment procedures.

A careful balance must be struck between judicial independence on the one hand and judicial monitoring, accountability and discipline on the other. Federal judges seem to have the most independence given the nature of their appointments.

PRACTICE TEST BANK

Multiple Choice

1. Federal judges serve _____.
    a. ten year terms
    b. life terms
    c. five year terms
    d. six year terms

2. The average salary of trial judges of general jurisdiction is _____.
    a. $60,000
    b. $80,000
    c. $100,000
    d. $120,000

3. Which of the following Supreme Court decisions first established guidelines for media coverage of trials?
    a. *Sheppard v. Maxwell*
    b. *Tennessee v. Garner*
    c. *Mapp v. Ohio*
    d. *Miranda v. Arizona*

4. The term "downward departures" means _____.
    a. harsh sentencing among state judges under federal sentencing guidelines
    b. harsh sentencing among federal judges under federal sentencing guidelines
    c. lenient sentencing among federal judges under federal sentencing guidelines
    d. lenient sentencing among state judges under federal sentencing guidelines

5. Two possibilities for improving the quality of the judiciary system are mechanisms for removing unfit judges and _____.
    a. merit selection
    b. political selection
    c. legislative selection
    d. seniority selection

6. Traditionally, judges enjoy the distinct benefits of _____.
    a. limited case loads
    b. higher salaries
    c. prestige and respect
    d. nine to five jobs

7. One method of selecting judges during the early Republic was by _____.
   a. a public vote
   b. executive appointment
   c. selection by judges
   d. allowing only those who practiced law to become a judge

8. More than half of all states select judges through _____.
   a. executive appointments
   b. judicial elections
   c. legislative appointments
   d. American Bar Association elections

9. The Supreme Court ruled that candidates for judicial office are free to announce their views on key issues in _____.
   a. *Bush v. Vera*
   b. *Miller v. Johnson*
   c. *Republican Party v. White*
   d. *U. S. v. Lanier*

10. The judicial conduct commission is designed to _____.
    a. investigate allegations against judicial misconduct
    b. investigate allegations against defense attorneys
    c. investigate allegations against probation officers
    d. investigate allegations against prosecutors

11. An increasing number of federal court vacancies have been filled by women and minorities since the presidency of whom?
    a. Bill Clinton
    b. Ronald Reagan
    c. Teddy Roosevelt
    d. Jimmy Carter

12. Prior to the 1980s, how many federal judges had been removed from office?
    a. 4
    b. 25
    c. 40
    d. 75

13. "Judge shopping" in multi-judge courts illustrates how judges _____.
    a. work together to establish symmetric sentencing
    b. differ in terms of sentences handed out
    c. work together to handle all case loads equally
    d. differ in terms of who will handle what cases

14. The U. S. Constitution specifies that the president has the power to nominate judges with the _____.
    a. advice of the judicial conduct commission
    b. advice of the U. S. House of Representatives
    c. advice of the U. S. Senate
    d. advice of the Supreme Court

15. Judges are typically _____.
    a. white, female, upper class, educated individuals
    b. white, male, lower class, uneducated individuals
    c. white, male, upper middle class, educated individuals
    d. white, female, middle class, educated individuals

16. Black judges are more likely to be found in states using _____.
    a. partisan election
    b. merit selection
    c. nonpartisan election
    d. appointment

17. The Voting Rights Act of 1965, amended in 1982, was found by the Supreme Court to apply to judicial elections in _____.
    a. *Powell v. Alabama*
    b. *Chisom v. Roemer*
    c. *Shaw v. Hunt*
    d. *Abrams et al. v. Johnson et al*

18. Which state became the first to adopt judicial conduct commissions to discipline judges?
    a. New York
    b. Missouri
    c. California
    d. Texas

19. The first woman to serve on the U. S. Supreme Court is/was _____.
    a. Sandra Day O' Connor
    b. Ruth Bader Ginsburg
    c. Harriet O' Neill
    d. Loretta Biggs

20. Research shows that women judges tend to be the strongest supporters of _____.
    a. lenient sentencing guidelines
    b. alternative methods to imprisonment
    c. women's rights claims
    d. lenient towards repeat minority offenders

True-False

1.   Judges have the authority to set bail and revoke it.
     a.   true
     b.   false

2.   One of the most frustrating aspects of being a judge is the heavy caseload.
     a.   true
     b.   false

3.   "Judge shopping" allows for lawyers to pick a judge that may be most favorable to their clients' case.
     a.   true
     b.   false

4.   When a judicial vacancy occurs, interim selection methods are commonly used.
     a.   true
     b.   false

5.   The crime control model calls for sentences based on rehabilitation.
     a.   true
     b.   false

6.   Jurors are the only ones who can legally determine if a person is guilty or innocent in trails.
     a.   true
     b.   false

7.   The public believes that judges are the principal decision makers in the courts.
     a.   true
     b.   false

8.   Judges are not considered as part of the courtroom group.
     a.   true
     b.   false

9.   Judges are influenced both directly and indirectly by other courthouse actors and broader trends in society.
     a.   true
     b.   false

10. Incumbent judges are rarely voted out of office.
     a.   true
     b.   false

11. Complaints and investigations against judges are confidential unless it is necessary to seek reprimand or serious sanctions.
    a. true
    b. false

12. Those who are impeached have commonly been convicted of the allegations against them.
    a. true
    b. false

13. The judicial conduct commission consists of judges, lawyers, and prominent laypersons.
    a. true
    b. false

14. Gubernatorial appointments are a method of judicial selection in which the governor appoints a person to a judicial vacancy without an election.
    a. true
    b. false

15. The merit selection of judges is believed to produce the best judges.
    a. true
    b. false

Fill in the Blank

1. The private offices of judges are referred to as _____ .

2. The _____ holds the judge most responsible for insuring that the criminal justice system operates fairly and impartially.

3. _____ courtesy refers to the expectation of Senators to be consulted before the president nominates a person for a judicial vacancy in their state.

4. Merit selection is commonly referred to as the _____ Bar Plan.

5. The due process model bases sentencing on _____ .

6. In addition to formal powers, judges also carry considerable _____ powers to fill court positions with friends, family, or political allies.

7. The Senate _____ Committee holds a hearing on presidential judicial nominees before the full Senate confirms them.

8. All Article _____ judges are selected by executive appointment.

9. _____ percent of federal judges had prior governmental experience.

10.   In the case, *Gregory v.* _____, the Supreme Court ruled that states requiring judges to retire at age seventy are not violating the federal Age Discrimination in Employment Act.

11.   Article _____ provides for the removal of civil officers of the United States, including federal judges, for certain crimes.

12.   The trial on the articles of impeachment is conducted before the _____.

13.   Corruption is included in the term judicial _____.

14.   _____ elections allow for the nominee's political party to be listed on the ballot.

15.   _____ does not mean conviction, but rather allegations of wrongdoing, roughly equivalent to a grand jury indictment.

Essay

1.   Explain the three major methods of judicial selection and give an example of each.

2.   Describe the characteristics of the traditional American judge. How has this changed today?

3.   Explain the judge's role in the courtroom work group.

4.   Explain the rationales for judicial independence and judicial accountability.

5.   Compare and contrast the state and federal systems for dealing with complaints about and disciplining errant judges.

CHAPTER 8 ANSWER KEYS

<u>Multiple Choice</u>

1—b	2—c	3—a	4—c	5—a
6—c	7—b	8—b	9—c	10—a
11—d	12—a	13—b	14—c	15—c
16—d	17—b	18—b	19—a	20—c

<u>True-False</u>

1—T	2—T	3—T	4—T	5—F
6—F	7—T	8—F	9—T	10—T
11—T	12—F	13—T	14—T	15—F

<u>Fill in the blank</u>

1—chambers	2—public	3—senatorial	4—Missouri
5—rehabilitation	6—patronage	7—Judiciary	8—III
9—80	10—*Ashcroft*	11—II	12—Senate
13—misconduct	14—Partisan	15—Impeachment	

Chapter 9
DEFENDANTS AND VICTIMS

LEARNING OBJECTIVES

After reading this chapter, student should understand the
- nature and characteristics of criminal defendants.
- anguish of crime victims.
- frustrations of victims in dealing with the criminal justice process.
- characteristics of crime victims.
- nature of victim and defendant relationships.
- evaluation of various victim/witness assistance programs.
- nature and extent of victims rights movements.

CHAPTER OUTLINE

I. **Defendants**
    A. Characteristics of Defendants
        1. Overwhelmingly male
        2. Women are less likely to be arrested compared to men
        3. Urban underclass
        4. Disproportionately members of racial minorities
    B. Defendants in Court
        1. Poor and uneducated
        2. Unfavorable attitudes toward the law

II. **Courts Through the Eyes of Victims and Witnesses**
    A. Frustrations in Coping with the Process
        1. As prosecutorial dominance increased, victim power decreased
        2. Trial delays result in frequent travel and wasted time
        3. Long waits in uncomfortable surroundings
        4. Lost wages for time spent in court
        5. Fear of defendant retaliation
        6. Lack of sympathy from justice officials
    B. Travails of Testifying
        1. Many victims feel as if they are on trial
        2. Rape trial trauma can be significant
    C. Surprising Support for the System
        1. Despite problems and frustrations, most victims and witnesses still express overall support for the court process

III. **Victims and Witnesses Through the Eyes of the Court**
    A. Lack of Cooperation
        1. Many victims and witnesses are reluctant to become involved in the criminal justice process
        2. More than half of all major crimes are never reported to police

3.   Noncooperative witnesses not always notified by prosecutors or police

B.   Characteristics of Victims

     1.   Young, non-white males, divorced or never married, low income, and unemployed

C.   Prior Relationships between Defendants and Victims

     1.   Roughly half of all violent crimes are committed by someone known by the victim such as relatives, friends, or acquaintances

D.   Domestic Violence

     1.   Women are the victims in 85% of all domestic violence incidents

     2.   Women are six times more likely than men to experience violence committed by an intimate

     3.   Research has found mixed results for the effectiveness of arrest on reducing domestic violence

     4.   Civil sanctions can also be used to combat domestic violence

IV.   Aiding Victims and Witnesses

A.   The Victim and Witness Act (1982) required greater protection and fair treatment for victims and witnesses in federal cases

B.   The Victims of Crime Act (1984) authorized the used of federal funds for state victim programs

C.   There are three common types of initiatives:

     1.   Victim/witness assistance

     2.   Victim compensation

     3.   Victims' bills of rights

A.   Victim/Witness Assistance Programs

     1.   Programs encourage cooperation in the prosecution of criminals by reducing inconveniences

          a.   Provide secure and comfortable waiting areas

          b.   Assist with recovering stolen property

          c.   Provide crisis intervention

          d.   Help victims understand the criminal justice process

          e.   Notify victims and witnesses of upcoming court dates

     2.   Evaluations of these programs have yielded mixed results

B.   Victim Compensation Programs

     1.   Most criminal defendants have no money to pay for personal or property damages

     2.   The rationale for compensation programs is that the government should counterbalance the losses suffered by victims due to criminal acts

     3.   The Victims of Crime Act (1984) established the Crime Victims Fund, financed primarily by fines paid in federal courts

C.   Victim's Bill of Rights

     1.   One view is premised on protecting the rights of victims and not defendants through significant law reforms

          a.   Abolishing the exclusionary rule

          b.   Limiting bail

          c.   Restricting plea bargaining

      d.   Imposing harsher punishment

    2.   The other popular view emphasizes improvements in court procedures to accommodate victims and witnesses, such as the National Conference of the Judiciary on the Rights of Victims of Crime: Statement of Recommended Judicial Practices

        a.   Fair treatment of victims and witnesses through better information about court procedures

        b.   Victim participation and input at all stages of judicial proceedings.

        c.   Better protection of victims from harassment, threats, intimidation, and harm

V.   Aiding or Manipulating Victims?

    A.   The Victims' Rights Movement

        1.   Victim advocacy groups have become a powerful political voice

           a.   Mothers Against Drunk Driving (MADD)

           b.   National Organization of Victim Assistance

    B.   Differing Goals

        1.   Polarized views on helping victims and punishing defendants

    C.   Do Victims Benefit?

        1.   Expense of programs and effectiveness of programs are at issue

        2.   The plight for victims' rights represents the historical conflict between the due process model and crime control model

VI.   Conclusion

KEY TERMS

civil protection order - Court order requiring a person to stay away from another person. (195)

defendant - The person or party against whom a lawsuit or prosecution is brought. (189)

CHAPTER SUMMARY

Victims and defendants are key elements in the criminal justice system. Arguably, without victims or witnesses, there would be no need for such a system. Historically, the justice system has focused more on defendants. We know much more about defendants and their rights than we do about victims and their rights.

As the majority of the research on crime leads back to defendants, we know much about them. Typical felony defendants are significantly younger, overwhelmingly male, less educated, likely to be unemployed, likely to be unwed, and disproportionately members of racial minorities and the urban underclass. While the defendant is supposed to stand at the center of the court process, most defendants are powerless due to poor education and little ability to help their own cause.

Traditionally, victims and witnesses have been forgotten players in the criminal justice process. In early America, victims played a key role in the justice system. However, as crimes came to be viewed as wrongs against the state and as prosecutorial dominance increased, the victims' role quickly began to decline. Today victims face numerous hardships in bringing their assailants to justice and often feel as if they have been ignored by the courts. Compared to defendants, there is a great lack of knowledge concerning victims and witnesses.

In general, victims are likely to have similar characteristics to their defendants and are also likely to have had a prior relationship with the defendant as well. Victim cooperation also plays a key role in the justice system, as increased victim cooperation increases the odds that a prosecutor will pursue a case. However, many victims and witnesses are reluctant to seek criminal sanctions due to a variety of reasons.

With the proliferation of the law and order and women's rights movements came the victims' rights movement, which led to a plethora of federal law concerning victims' rights, such as the Victim and Witness Protection Act (1982) and the Victims of Crime Act(1984). This federal legislation spawned victims' rights legislation throughout the nation and resulted in three main types of victim initiatives: victim/witness assistance programs, victim compensation programs, and victims' bills of rights. Most if not all states have some form of victims' rights and victim assistance programs.

Several victims' rights organizations have made serious inroads and are becoming important political forces. Mothers Against Drunk Driving (MADD) is one of the most influential.

A Victims' Rights Amendment to the U.S. Constitution was debated in Congress but not approved for submission to the states. The topic of victims' rights has been and remains very controversial, as even different victims' rights organizations disagree on philosophies and goals concerning this topic. Nevertheless, the victims' rights movement is at the forefront of court reform.

PRACTICE TEST BANK

Multiple Choice

1. Most defendants are primarily _____.
   a. female, young, white, and middle class
   b. female, young, minority, and lower class
   c. male, young, white, and middle class
   d. male, young, minority, and lower class

2. In the U.S., roughly _____ of all violent crimes are committed by family members, friends, or acquaintances.
   a. one fourth
   b. one third
   c. half
   d. two thirds

3. The Supreme Court ruled in _____ that the characteristics of the victim are irrelevant during death penalty deliberations.
   a. Booth v. Maryland
   b. Payne v. Tennessee
   c. South Carolina v. Gathers
   d. Gerstein v. Pugh

4. According to the Bureau of Justice Statistics, the greatest percentage of _____ are committed by someone who knows the victim.
   a. thefts
   b. burglaries
   c. homicides
   d. arsons

5. The first state to start a victim compensation program in the U.S. was _____.
   a. New York
   b. Texas
   c. California
   d. Florida

6. Civil protection orders provide many victims with _____.
   a. a false sense of security
   b. security against their attackers
   c. monetary support
   d. assistance in dealing with the grueling court process

7. The largest victim advocacy group is _____.
    a. SADD
    b. MADD
    c. USAA
    d. Candle Lighters of America

8. The Supreme Court ruled that the Eighth Amendment does not prohibit the sentencing jury in capital cases from considering the victims impact statement in _____.
    a. *Booth v. Maryland*
    b. *South Carolina v. Gathers*
    c. *Vermont v. Grace*
    d. *Payne v. Tennessee*

9. The criminal justice system is considered to be primarily _____.
    a. offender-oriented
    b. victim-oriented
    c. offender and victim-oriented
    d. law enforcement-oriented

10. The maximum amount that is paid for damages by victim's compensation programs is generally between _____.
    a. $5,000 to $10,000
    b. $10,000 to $25,000
    c. $50,000 to $75,000
    d. $75,000 to $100,000

11. Advocacy groups for victims seek to _____.
    a. provide support for victims and defendants alike
    b. provide only financial support to victims
    c. project the interests of crime victims into the mainstream of American political discourse
    d. provide a voice to defendants as well as victims

12. _____ have provided little influence over the outcome of cases they are involved in.
    a. Defendants
    b. Lawyers
    c. Advocacy groups
    d. Victims

13. About _____ incidents of intimate violence occur each year.
    a. 700,000
    b. 750,000
    c. 800,000
    d. 825,000

14. The _____, passed in 1982, required greater protection of victims and witnesses and mandated guidelines for fair treatment in federal criminal cases.
     a.   Victims of Crime Act
     b.   Antiterrorism and Effective Death Penalty Act
     c.   Victim and Witness Protection Act
     d.   President's Task Force on Victims of Crime

15. The _____ established a crime victims' fund, which is primarily financed from fines paid by defendants in federal court.
     a.   Victims of Crime Act
     b.   Antiterrorism and Effective Death Penalty Act
     c.   Victims' Bill of Rights
     d.   Victim and Witness Protection Act

16. In _____ cases, police officers have a difficult time due to the prior relationship between the victim and the offender.
     a.   homicide
     b.   assault
     c.   robbery
     d.   domestic violence

17. New York's "Son of Sam" law was found unconstitutional in _____.
     a.   *Payne v. Tennessee*
     b.   *Simon & Schuster v. New York State Crime Victims Board*
     c.   *Booth v. Maryland*
     d.   *New York State Crime Victims Board v. Jackson*

18. Some states have a "family exclusion" clause that _____.
     a.   does not allow victims, living in the same household as the offender, to be eligible for financial assistance
     b.   allows for financial assistance to the victim's family
     c.   does not allow the offender to reside with the victim
     d.   allows the offender to receive assistance as well as the victim

19. _____ are commonly a powerful political voice for most victims.
     a.   Lawyers
     b.   Judges
     c.   Police officers
     d.   Advocacy groups

20. One in how many black males are either in prison, on probation, or on parole?
     a.   3
     b.   10
     c.   25
     d.   50

True-False

1. Most criminal defendants are female.
    a.   true
    b.   false

2. Victims and witnesses must endure several hardships while participating in the criminal justice process, including fear of the defendant or retaliation from the defendant's associates.
    a.   true
    b.   false

3. In today's criminal justice process victims play a prominent role.
    a.   true
    b.   false

4. Before the American Revolution, victims had little to do with the criminal justice system.
    a.   true
    b.   false

5. As prosecutorial dominance increased, the power of victims declined.
    a.   true
    b.   false

6. The criminal justice system in the United States is victim-oriented.
    a.   true
    b.   false

7. Before mandatory arrest policies, police officers commonly made arrests as a last resort in domestic violence cases.
    a.   true
    b.   false

8. Victim/witness assistance programs are intended to provide comfortable and secure waiting areas, assist with the return of recovered property, and crisis intervention.
    a.   true
    b.   false

9. After cross-examination, many witnesses or victims feel as if they had been put on trial.
    a.   true
    b.   false

10. The victim-defendant relationship has little influence on the outcome and processing of court cases.
    a.   true
    b.   false

11. Organizing crime victims is considered an easy task by most observers.
    a. true
    b. false

12. Victim advocacy groups have had very little political influence.
    a. true
    b. false

13. Nearly all major crimes are reported to police.
    a. true
    b. false

14. A small group of career criminals are responsible for a disproportionate amount of crime.
    a. true
    b. false

15. Evaluation of victim/witness assistance programs have yielded mixed results.
    a. true
    b. false

Fill in the Blank

1. The three most commonly discussed characteristics of defendants are gender, race, and _____.

2. Prior _____ are common in many cases of homicide and assault.

3. The Victim and _____ Protection Act required greater protection of victims and witnesses and also mandated guidelines for the fair treatment of victims and witnesses in federal criminal cases.

4. Typical felony defendants are predominantly drawn from what sociologists call the _____ underclass.

5. According to *Payne v. Tennessee*, the Supreme Court ruled that the Eighth Amendment creates no bar to the introduction of victim _____ statements during sentencing.

6. When crime became viewed as an offense against the state, the _____ was assigned a subordinate role.

7. Since many criminal defendants do not have the money to pay for damages, _____ cases are of little relevance.

8. Women in prison for crimes like robbery, burglary, and drug dealing were likely to have had a _____ accomplice who played a primary role.

9.   Minorities are imprisoned at significantly _____ rates than whites.

10.   More than _____ of all major crimes are never reported to the police.

11.   The criminal justice system in the United States is _____-oriented.

12.   Discussion over victim's bills of rights is the most recent example of conflict between the due _____ model and the crime control model.

13.   Victim/witness _____ programs encourage cooperation in the court process by reducing inconveniences faced by citizens appearing in court.

14.   The three most common types of help or initiatives victims can receive are assistance programs, victims' bill of rights, and victim _____ programs.

15.   Victim cooperation with the prosecution dramatically _____ the odds that a case will be prosecuted.

Essay

1.   Discuss the three common types of victim initiatives.

2.   Discuss some of the hardships endured by victims in the court process and also some of the problems they create for court officials.

3.   Describe the characteristics of the typical felony defendant. Are there any characteristics or relationships that have a bearing on the judicial process?

4.   Describe and explain the historical decline in victim power in the U.S.

5.   Discuss the advantages, disadvantages, and controversy surrounding the victims' bill of rights.

CHAPTER 9 ANSWER KEYS

Multiple Choice

1—d	2—c	3—c	4—c	5—c
6—a	7—b	8—d	9—a	10—b
11—c	12—d	13—a	14—c	15—a
16—d	17—b	18—a	19—d	20—a

True-False

1—F	2—T	3—F	4—F	5—T
6—F	7—T	8—T	9—T	10—F
11—F	12—F	13—F	14—F	15—T

Fill in the blank

1—poverty	2—relationships	3—Witness	4—urban
5—impact	6—victim	7—civil	8—male
9—higher	10—half	11—offender	12—process
13—assistance	14—compensation	15—increases	

Chapter 10
ARREST TO ARRAIGNMENT

LEARNING OBJECTIVES
After reading this chapter, students should understand the
- nature and extent of processing the accused through arrests.
- role and function of initial appearances.
- criminal court process of filing charges.
- role of prosecutors in the charging process.
- role and function of preliminary hearings.
- grand jury process.
- role and function of the arraignment process.
- nature and extent case attrition.
- wedding cake model of justice.

CHAPTER OUTLINE

I.   **Crime**
    A.   Decreased considerably since early 1990s
    B.   UCR: Type I offenses consist of eight types of serious index crimes
    C.   UCR: Type II offenses consist of less serious crimes
    D.   UCR data is based on reported crimes known to police

II.   **Arrest**
    A.   Only 21% of crimes known to the police result in an arrest
    B.   Every year, police make 13.7 million nontraffic arrests in which 2.2 million are for serious crimes
    C.   Quality of Arrests
        1.   Thoroughness of investigations related to arrests
    D.   Swelling Criminal Dockets
        1.   Prosecuted cases in federal court doubled between 1980 and 1998
        2.   Felony prosecutions increased 25 percent in state courts

III.   **Initial Appearance**
    A.   Occurs within a short period of the arrest
    B.   Most misdemeanor defendants enter a guilty plea and are sentenced at this stage

IV.   **Charging**
    A.   Elements (*Corpus Delecti*) must be specified in a formal document
        1.   Complaint
        2.   Information
        3.   Arrest warrant
    B.   Law on the Books: Prosecutorial Control
    C.   Law in Action: Police Influence
    D.   Law in Controversy: Should Prosecutors Set High Standards for Charging?

111

V.   Preliminary Hearing
   A.   Law on the Books: Weighing Probable Cause
      1.   Establishes probable cause and binds over the accused for trial or indictment
   B.   Law in Action: Variations in Using the Preliminary Hearing
      1.   Redundancy, damage to defendants case, client control, and overview of the states case against the defendant
      2.   Waiving preliminary hearings is largely ceremonial

VI.   Grand Jury
   A.   Impaneled to investigate and verify charges against a defendant
   B.   Law on the Books: Shield and Sword
      1.   Indictment or *true bill* issued when jury finds charges to be true
      2.   If charges are insufficient they return no bill or *no true bill*
      3.   Authority to investigate
         a.   Transactional immunity
         b.   Use immunity
         c.   subpoena power
   C.   Law in Action: Prosecutorial Domination
      1.   Grand juries often act as a rubber stamp for prosecutors
   D.   Law in Controversy: Reform the Grand Jury?
      1.   Grand juries as political ends
      2.   Advocates suggest witnesses should have right to counsel

VII. Arraignment
   A.   Informs defendant of charges and allows entering of plea

VIII. Law-in-Action Perspective: Case Attrition
   A.   Dismissal of cases in the early stages (*nolle prosequi*)

IX.   Why Attrition Occurs
   A.   Three facets of work group discretion affect case attrition
   B.   Legal Judgments
   C.   Policy Priorities
   D.   Personal Standards of Justice

X.   The Criminal Justice Wedding Cake
   A.   There are four levels of cases in the system that are handled differently
   B.   Celebrated Cases (layer 1)
      1.   Sensationalized cases that attract massive media attention
      2.   Cases are not commonly representative of the criminal justice system
   C.   Serious Felonies (layer 2)
      1.   Distinguished by courtroom work group as more serious than layer 3 cases
         a.   Seriousness of crime
         b.   Suspect's criminal record
         c.   Victim-offender relationship

D.   Lesser Felonies (layer 3)
1.   Routine cases viewed as garbage or not real crimes
2.   Receives cases downgraded from layers 1 and 2
E.   The Lower Depths (layer 4)
1.   Staggering volume of misdemeanors
a.   Least serious crimes
b.   About half are public order offenses

XI.   Conclusion
A.   Decisions made at early points of the process set the tone for cases moving through the criminal court process
B.   Decisions about innocence and guilt are made in early stages rather than from an adversarial system as projected by many observers

KEY TERMS

arraignment - The stage of the criminal process in which the defendant is formally told the charges and allowed to enter a plea. (211)

arrest - The physical taking into custody of a suspected law violator or juvenile. (210)

arrest warrant - A document issued by a judicial officer authorizing the arrest of a specific person. (213)

bind over - If at the preliminary hearing the judge believes that sufficient probable cause exists to hold a criminal defendant, the accused is said to be bound over for trial. (216)

charging document - An information, indictment, or complaint that states the formal criminal charge against a named defendant. (213)

complaint - In civil law, the first paper filed in a lawsuit. In criminal law, a charge signed by the victim that a person named has committed a specified offense. (213)

contempt of court - The failure or refusal to obey a court order; may be punished by a fine or imprisonment. (218)

grand jury - A group of citizens who decide whether persons accused of crimes should be indicted (true bill) or not (no true bill). (216)

immunity - A grant of exemption from prosecution in return for evidence or testimony. (217)

index crimes - The specific crimes used by the FBI when reporting the incidence of crime in the United States in the *Uniform Crime Reports*. (208)

indictment - A formal accusation of a criminal offense made against a person by a grand jury. (217)

information - A formal accusation charging someone with the commission of a crime, signed by a prosecuting attorney, which has the effect of bringing the person to trial. (213)

initial appearance - Shortly after arrest, the suspect is brought before a judicial official who informs the person of the reason for the arrest and, in the case of a felony, sets bond. (212)

no true bill - The decision of a grand jury not to indict a person for a crime. (217)

nolle prosequi - The ending of a criminal case because the prosecutor decides or agrees to stop prosecuting. When this happens, the case is "nollied," "nolled," or "nol. prossed." (220)

preliminary hearing - A pretrial hearing to determine whether there is probable cause to hold the accused for the grand jury. (214)

probable cause - Standard used to determine whether a crime has been committed and whether there is sufficient evidence to believe a specific individual committed it. (216)

subpoena (power) - An order from a court directing a person to appear before the court and to give testimony about a cause of action pending before it. (218)

transactional immunity - Absolute protection against prosecution for any event or transaction about which a witness is compelled to give testimony or furnish evidence. (217)

true bill - A bill of indictment by a grand jury. (217)

Type I offenses - Serious crimes of homicide, rape, arson, aggravated assault, robbery, burglary, auto theft, and larceny, according to the FBI's *Uniform Crime Reports*; also called *index crimes*. (208)

use immunity - A witness may not be prosecuted based on grand jury testimony he or she provides but may be prosecuted based on evidence acquired independently from that testimony. (218)

CHAPTER SUMMARY

The Uniform Crime Report is an annual FBI publication of crime and is the most widely-known measure of crime. Crimes are broken down into two categories. Type I offenses or index crimes are made up of eight serious types of crimes. Type II offenses consists of lesser and more numerous crimes. A major weakness of the UCR is that the information is based only on crimes known or reported to police, in which case the UCR drastically underestimates crime. Despite public perceptions, crime has been on the decrease since the early 1990s.

Only about 21% of crimes known to the police result in an arrest (clearance rate). The clearance rate for violent crimes is roughly 50%, while that for property crimes is 18%. The recovery of tangible evidence by the officer or the presence of a cooperative witness significantly enhances the probability of conviction. Furthermore, it has been found that some police agencies conduct more thorough investigations than others.

There are four basic types of charging documents used in the criminal justice system: complaint, information, arrest warrant, and grand jury indictments. All provide a brief description, the date, and location of the offense; and all are based on probable cause or the equivalent. A complaint is supported by oath or affirmation by the victim or arresting officer. Complaints are generally used for misdemeanors and ordinance violations.

A formal information is almost identical to a complaint except that it must be signed by the prosecutor and is used in lieu of a grand jury for felonies in states that do not have grand juries. For grand jury states, the information is used to initiate grand jury proceedings. An indictment is a finding of evidence of wrongdoing or a crime, necessitating a trial. An arrest warrant is issued by a judicial officer, generally a lower court judge, and states the charges against the suspect.

The initial appearance occurs within a short time of arrest and is the stage at which most misdemeanor defendants enter a guilty plea and are sentenced immediately. A preliminary hearing is the first hearing for felony defendants, in which probable cause is ascertained by a lower court judge or magistrate. According to *County of Riverside v. McLaughlin*, an individual may be jailed up to forty-eight hours before seeing a magistrate. During a preliminary hearing, prosecutors need only establish probable cause that a crime has been committed and that the defendant committed the crime, not proof beyond a reasonable doubt necessary for conviction.

Grand juries are provided for in the 5th Amendment. However, they are used to varying degrees in different states. There are a number of differences between grand juries and trial juries. Grand juries make accusations, while trial juries decide actual guilt or innocence. Grand jury proceedings are held in secrecy to protect individuals under mere suspicion and generally only a plurality vote is necessary to return an indictment. An indictment is a finding of enough evidence or probable cause to proceed with a trial. The return of an indictment is also known as a true bill. Witnesses and suspects before grand juries have fewer rights than in the trial courts and suspects don't even have the right to present their version of the facts. The prosecutor is charged with supervising the grand jury, but in reality, grand juries generally act as a rubber stamp for the prosecutor.

Grand juries also have the ability to grant immunity from prosecution in order to persuade witnesses to testify. Transactional immunity was the initial type of immunity used, but use immunity is also common and provides less protection for witnesses than transactional immunity.

Arraignment occurs in trial courts of general jurisdiction and is the stage in which the defendant is formally charged and asked to enter a plea. Defendants that reach the arraignment stage generally have a high presumption of guilt.

Overall, only fifty-five out of one hundred cases make it to the trial stage. This loss of cases from arrest to arraignment is known as case attrition. The three facets of discretion of the courtroom work group: legal judgments, policy priorities, and personal standards of justice; and thus the courtroom work group itself, play a major role in case attrition.

Samuel Walker's criminal justice wedding cake model is based on and demonstrates the premise that criminal justice officials receive and handle different types of cases in different fashions. Celebrated cases make up the top layer of the cake, as they receive the most media attention, but only account for a very small percentage of criminal justice cases. Serious felonies make up the second layer of the cake, while the less serious, but more numerous lesser felonies make up the third layer. The fourth layer consists of the numerous misdemeanors and lesser crimes, and processes the most cases within the system.

PRACTICE TEST BANK

Multiple Choice

1. Which of the following is a major weakness of the Uniform Crime Report?
    a. The data is only available for some states.
    b. It is based only on crimes reported to police.
    c. The data is only published every ten years.
    d. It only reports federal crimes.

2. The most publicized measure of crime is _____.
    a. the Uniform Crime Report
    b. the arrest reports for each state
    c. the number of convictions given
    d. the number of arrests that lead to convictions

3. Only _____ of crimes reported to the police lead to an arrest.
    a. 5 percent
    b. 21 percent
    c. 55 percent
    d. 76 percent

4. The stage at which the defendant enters their plea of guilty in most misdemeanor cases is during the_____.
    a. grand jury
    b. preliminary hearing
    c. initial appearance
    d. indictment

5. The _____ decides what charges should be filed in court.
    a. prosecutor
    b. defense attorney
    c. judge
    d. police officer

6. In the Supreme Court case of _____, the Court held that states have the option of using either an indictment or an information.
    a. *Campbell v. Florida*
    b. *Hurtado v. California*
    c. *County of Riverside v. Mclaughlin*
    d. *Cousin v. Small*

7.   In *County of Riverside v. McLaughlin*, the Court held that a preliminary hearing must be held within how many hours of arrest?
   a.   24
   b.   36
   c.   48
   d.   60

8.   A journalist must testify before a grand jury according to the Supreme Court ruling in
   _____.
   a.   *U.S. v. Williams*
   b.   *Campbell v. Louisiana*
   c.   *Branzburg v. Hayes*
   d.   *Hurtado v. California*

9.   The leading advocate for federal grand jury reform is _____.
   a.   the National Association of Criminal Defense Lawyers
   b.   the American Bar Association
   c.   the Department of Criminal Justice
   d.   the National Commission on Law Observance and Enforcement

10.   Under the _____ Amendment, "no person shall be held to answer for a capital, or otherwise infamous crime, unless on a presentment or indictment of a grand jury."
   a.   Third
   b.   Fourth
   c.   Fifth
   d.   Sixth

11.   The burden of proof required in a preliminary hearing is _____.
   a.   proof beyond a reasonable doubt
   b.   preponderance of evidence
   c.   reasonable suspicion
   d.   probable cause

12.   The "Wedding Cake" model contains _____ layers.
   a.   one
   b.   two
   c.   three
   d.   four

13.   For every 100 arrests, _____ are rejected, diverted, or referred to other jurisdictions during prosecutorial screening.
   a.   15
   b.   24
   c.   30
   d.   32

14.   The clearance rate for violent crimes is about _____ percent.
    a.   20
    b.   30
    c.   40
    d.   50

15.   A(n) _____ must be supported by oath or affirmation of either the victim or the arresting officer.
    a.   subpoena
    b.   complaint
    c.   information
    d.   indictment

16.   Arraignment commonly occurs in which type of court?
    a.   trial courts of limited jurisdiction
    b.   trial courts of general jurisdiction
    c.   appellate courts
    d.   courts of last resort

17.   When the grand jury decides that there is enough evidence to hold a suspect for trial, they return an indictment or _____.
    a.   complaint
    b.   true bill
    c.   no true bill
    d.   information

18.   Which of the following is not considered within the authority of a grand jury?
    a.   to convict defendants
    b.   to subpoena witnesses
    c.   to indict defendants
    d.   to grant witnesses immunity

19.   Which of the following terms is not among the types of charging documents?
    a.   arrest warrant
    b.   complaint
    c.   indictment
    d.   *corpus delicti*

20.   In which of the following decisions did the Court rule that the government is under no obligation to disclose evidence to the grand jury that may help clear the suspect or defendant?
    a.   *Roe v. Wade*
    b.   *Terry v. Ohio*
    c.   *Burns v. Reed*
    d.   *U.S. v. Williams*

True-False

1. White-collar crimes are primarily committed by the middle class.
    a.   true
    b.   false

2. On average, police arrest close to half a million individuals for serious crimes, such as murder, rape, and arson.
    a.   true
    b.   false

3. An information document is commonly used in prosecuting misdemeanor offenses.
    a.   true
    b.   false

4. The prosecutor's signature is the only difference between the information and the complaint documents.
    a.   true
    b.   false

5. A preliminary hearing is to determine if there is sufficient probable cause to keep the suspect/accused for further proceedings.
    a.   true
    b.   false

6. A return of no *true bill* means that the court finds the charges against a suspect to be sufficient.
    a.   true
    b.   false

7. The United States has a higher crime rate than any other Western industrial democracy.
    a.   true
    b.   false

8. Use immunity provides more protection than does transactional immunity.
    a.   true
    b.   false

9. The top layer of the criminal justice "Wedding Cake" model contains the fewest number of cases.
    a.   true
    b.   false

10. The criminal justice "Wedding Cake" model is based on the observation that criminal justice system processes cases differently.
    a.   true
    b.   false

11. Usually hearsay evidence is admissible during preliminary hearings.
    a.   true
    b.   false

12. When an individual fails to comply with a subpoena, he or she is in contempt of court.
    a.   true
    b.   false

13. Property crimes are more likely to be cleared by police than violent crimes.
    a.   true
    b.   false

14. An indictment is an informal accusation of a crime.
    a.   true
    b.   false

15. An arrest warrant is commonly issued by the arresting officer.
    a.   true
    b.   false

Fill in the Blank

1. Drug crimes are considered or counted as Type _____ offenses.

2. The Uniform Crime Reports are statistically weak in that they are based only on crimes known to the _____.

3. The physical taking of a suspected law violator into custody is considered an _____.

4. The charging _____ contains a short/ brief description of the date and location of the offense.

5. An arrest _____ is issued by a judicial officer.

6. Type I offenses of the UCR are also referred to as _____ crimes.

7. When a prosecutor agrees not to prosecute the witness for any crimes admitted in exchange for their testimony, they are granting _____.

8.   Three criteria that explain case attrition are legal judgments, personal standards of justice, and _____ priorities.

9.   _____ judgments are the most important reason for case attrition

10.   The O.J. Simpson case is an example of a _____ case, which is the top layer of the criminal justice "Wedding Cake" model.

11.   Grand juries generally indict whoever the _____ wants indicted.

12.   When a prosecutor dismisses a case it is considered no prosecution or_____ _____.

13.   When a grand jury requires an individual to appear before them, they are enacting their _____power.

14.   Under _____ immunity, the government may not use a witness's testimony to prosecute that individual, but may prosecute the witness based on other independently obtained evidence.

15.   A prosecutor must establish _____ cause that a crime has been committed and that the defendant committed it in order to successfully charge a defendant.

Essay

1.   Briefly explain the four types of charging documents.

2.   Explain the differences between the proceedings of a grand jury and a regular trial jury.

3.   Explain the two types of immunity and their differences.

4.   Explain the criminal justice wedding cake model.

5.   Discuss case attrition and why it occurs.

CHAPTER 10 ANSWER KEYS

Multiple Choice

1—b	2—a	3—b	4—c	5—a
6—b	7—c	8—c	9—a	10—c
11—d	12—d	13—b	14—d	15—b
16—b	17—b	18—a	19—d	20—d

True-False

1—F	2—F	3—F	4—T	5—T
6—F	7—T	8—F	9—T	10—T
11—T	12—T	13—F	14—F	15—F

Fill in the blank

1—II	2—police	3—arrest	4—document
5—warant	6—index	7—immunity	8—priorities
9—Legal	10—celebrated	11—prosecutor	12—*nolle prosequi*
13—subpoena	14—use	15—probable	

Chapter 11
BAIL

After reading this chapter, students should understand the

- various forms of bail and bail procedures.
- factors that affect setting of bail.
- process of setting bail.
- role of bail bondsmen.
- effects of the bail system.
- various attempts at reforming the bail process.

CHAPTER OUTLINE

I. **Law on the Books: The Monetary Bail System**
   A. Bail Procedures
   B. Forms of Bail
      1. Cash bond
      2. Property bond
      3. Release on recognizance
      4. Bail agent/bondsman
   C. Conflicting Theories of Bail
      1. Due process model
      2. Crime control model

II. **Law in Action: The Context of Bail Setting**
   A. Uncertainty
   B. Risk
      1. Defendant may commit a crime while on bail
      2. Type 1 and 2 errors
   C. Jail Overcrowding
      1. As jails become overcrowded, bail-setting practices become more lenient

III. **The Process of Bail Setting**
   A. Seriousness of the Crime
   B. Prior Criminal Record
   C. Situational Justice

IV. **Bail Bondsmen**
   A. The Business Setting
      1. Bail bonding as a business with a 10% fee for assuming the risk of the bond
   B. Bail Bondsmen and the Courtroom Work Group
      1. Bondsmen help to manage the population of arrested persons

V.   **Effects of the Bail System**
    A.   Race and Ethnicity
          1.   Hispanics most likely to be disparaged by bail
    B.   Failure to Appear
          1.   Only about 6 percent of released defendants fail to appear
    C.   Case Disposition
          1.   Jailed defendants are more likely to be sentenced to prison

VI.   **Bail Reform Based on the Due Process Model**
    A.   The Bail Reform Act of 1966 created a presumption favoring pretrial release
    B.   Ten Percent Bail Deposit
    C.   Pretrial Service Programs

VII.   **Bail Reform Based on the Crime Control Model**
    A.   The Bail Reform Act of 1984 authorizes preventative detention
    B.   Pretrial Crimes
          1.   Pretrial service programs help to assess risk.
    C.   Preventative Detention
          1.   Prevent pretrial crimes and protect communities

VIII. **Conclusion**

KEY TERMS

bail - The security (money or bail bond) given as a guarantee that a released prisoner will appear at trial. (230)

bail agent (bail bondsman) - A person whose business it is to effect release on bail for persons held in custody by pledging to pay a sum of money if a defendant fails to appear in court as required. (231)

bench warrant (**capias**) - An order issued by the court itself, or from the bench, for the arrest of a person; it is not based, as is an arrest warrant, on a probable cause showing that a person has committed a crime, but only on the person's failure to appear in court as directed. (238)

cash bond - Requirement that money be posted to secure pretrial release. (230)

preventive detention - Holding a defendant in custody pending trial in the belief that he or she is likely to commit further criminal acts or flee the jurisdiction. (242)

property bond - Use of property as collateral for pretrial release. (230)

release on recognizance (**ROR**) - The release of an accused person from jail on his or her own obligation rather than on a monetary bond. (230)

CHAPTER SUMMARY

The right to bail is guaranteed in the 8th Amendment of the U.S. Constitution. However, the practice of allowing defendants to be released prior to trial originated in England. The right to bail, like anything else, also has limitations. There are four basic ways in which a defendant may be released prior to trial: cash bond, property bond, release on recognizance, and through a bail agent.

In posting a cash bond, the defendant pays the full bond amount out of pocket. However, this type of bail is rarely used, as few people possess the ability to raise large amounts of money quickly. Defendants may also post a property bond by using a piece of property as collateral. This type of bail is also rare, as few defendants possess the property necessary for bail. Furthermore, courts generally require that the equity of the property equal double the amount of the bond. The third type of bond is release on recognizance, in which the judge will release defendants with strong ties to the community or low flight risk without monetary bail. The most common type of bail is that posted through a bail agent.

Bail agents act as a type of insurance, in that they will post bail for clients for a nonrefundable 10% fee. To protect their interests, bail agents will purchase a surety bond from insurance companies, who normally charge 30% of the bondsman's fee. Bondsmen will not post bail for everyone, as they prefer clients with low bail amounts and low flight risks. In assessing risks and choosing clients, bondsmen help the courts control the arrested jail population. On any given day, there are more than 750,000 people in jail, half of which have not been convicted of any crime.

In assessing risk and financial ability, bondsmen look at the defendant's family situation, employment history, and ties to the community. Bondsmen consider first-time offenders, recidivists with increasingly more serious crimes, and violent defendants as bad risks for bail. While bail bonding is a private business, they also play an important role in the court systems, and thus maintain a reciprocal relationship with the courts. Judges often reciprocate a bail bondsman's cooperation with the courtroom work group by not collecting forfeited bail.

Bondsmen also possess a unique ability in apprehending bail jumpers: the use of bail enforcement agents. Bail enforcement agents, or bounty hunters, face less restriction than law enforcement officials and can retrieve fugitives much easier than law officials. Such means have proven rather effective.

The context of court bail setting revolves around three factors: uncertainty, risk, and jail overcrowding. In determining bail, judges and other official may make two types of mistakes: Type 1 or Type 2 errors. A Type 1 error occurs when a judge releases a defendant who commits a crime while on bail. A Type 2 error occurs when a judge detains a defendant who should have been released. Judges mainly face criticism for Type 1 errors. Prison overcrowding plays an important role, as it is a principal cause of jail overcrowding. As jails become overcrowded, bail-setting practices become more lenient.

Trial court judges have virtually unlimited discretion in fixing bail and generally the higher the bail amount, the less likely a defendant is to make bail. In setting bail, judges look at two main factors: the seriousness of the crime and the defendant's prior criminal record. The seriousness of the crime is the most important, and as the seriousness of the crime increases, so does the bail amount. Additionally, race and ethnicity impact the bail setting process with Hispanics being the most likely to be denied bail compared to Whites who are most likely to be granted bail. Defendants with a prior criminal record also face increased bail amounts. There is a general consensus that jailed defendants are more likely to be convicted and sentenced to prison than those who have been released prior to trial. However, the degree of this disparity remains unclear.

The Bail Reform Act of 1966 created a presumption favoring pretrial release consistent with the due process model. However, recent trends indicate a shift to the crime control model. The Bail Reform Act of 1984 authorized the use of pretrial or preventative detention and was upheld by the Supreme Court in *U.S. v. Salerno*. In that case the Court stated that the Eighth Amendment does not create a right to bail. It creates only a right to have bail set at a reasonable amount if the defendant is otherwise bailable. The 1984 act allows defendants to be held for up to ninety days without bail when there is evidence that it would better protect the community. Thus, while advocates of the due process model insist that the purpose of bail is to ensure that defendants appear for trial, crime control advocates believe that bail should also be used to protect society.

In estimating pretrial crime and nonappearance, an accurate estimate of those who fail to appear is 8%. As the time from arrest to trial increases, so does the rate of nonappearance. Regarding pretrial crimes, the rate of felonies committed while on bail is generally 5-7%.

Alternative approaches to bail agents is the use of pretrial service programs. In some jurisdictions, courts have cut out bail agents and administer the bail procedures themselves. Many of these courts use pretrial release programs to assess defendant bail risk. Supporters of such programs claim that nonappearance rates are lower and that the programs save money as opposed to the use of bail agents. Generally, such programs release the same people who would have made bail. While the current trend regarding the crime control model has changed procedures, it has had little overall impact on detention policies, as judges simply have another option in determining bail.

PRACTICE TEST BANK

Multiple Choice

1. When defendants are released from jail without a monetary bond, it is called _____.
    a. cash bond
    b. property bond
    c. release on recognizance
    d. bail bond

2. If bail is set at $20,000 and the defendant uses a bail agent, then the bail will only actually cost the defendant how much?
    a. $2,000
    b. $5,000
    c. $20,000
    d. $40,000

3. Generally, the most important factor in determining the amount of bail is _____.
    a. the defendant's prior record
    b. the seriousness of the offense
    c. the defendant's race
    d. the defendant's demeanor

4. Who issues a bench warrant?
    a. bail bondsmen
    b. prosecutors
    c. police
    d. judges

5. Which Amendment says that "excessive bail shall not be required?"
    a. First Amendment
    b. Fifth Amendment
    c. Eighth Amendment
    d. Ninth Amendment

6. In *U.S. v. Salerno*, the Supreme Court upheld which of the following?
    a. bail bonding
    b. pretrial release
    c. release on recognizance
    d. preventative detention

7. Defendants who are accused of which type of crime commonly have no right to bail?
    a. capital crimes
    b. rape
    c. burglary
    d. drug offenses

8. In general, the American bail system is based on a defendant's access to _____.
    a. a defense attorney
    b. friends in high places
    c. money
    d. a judge

9. Advocates of which justice model support the use of bail to protect society?
    a. adversarial model
    b. crime control model
    c. due process model
    d. criminal justice wedding cake model

10. In order to post a property bond on $20,000, the defendant's property must be worth how much?
    a. $2,000
    b. $5,000
    c. $20,000
    d. $40,000

11. Overall, pretrial crime rates have been found to be approximately _____.
    a. 1-3%
    b. 5-7%
    c. 20-22%
    d. 35-37%

12. Which of the following authorizes preventative detention for federal defendants accused of serious crimes?
    a. the Bail Reform Act of 1984
    b. the Victims of Crime Act of 1984
    c. the Bail Reform Act of 1966
    d. the Antiterrorism and Effective Death Penalty Act

13. Approximately how many jails are in the U.S.?
    a. 1,000
    b. 3,400
    c. 6,000
    d. 10,000

14. Which of the following ideologies refers to the belief that the meaning of the Constitution should be adjusted to meet the demands of a changing society?
    a. adaptationism
    b. strict constructionism
    c. antidisestablishmentarism
    d. libertarianism

15. Strict constructionism is a term usually associated with which political group?
    a. liberals
    b. conservatives
    c. libertarians
    d. Marxists

16. A principal reason for jail overcrowding since the 1980s has been _____.
    a. prison overcrowding
    b. preventative detention
    c. high bail amounts
    d. release on recognizance

17. Which of the four types of release is most commonly used in the criminal justice system?
    a. cash bond
    b. property bond
    c. release on recognizance
    d. bail bondsmen

18. Supporters of _____ model believe that the only purpose of bail is to ensure that the defendant appears in court for trial?
    a. adversarial
    b. crime control
    c. due process
    d. criminal justice wedding cake

19. Which of the following is credited with first developing and testing the pretrial service programs?
    a. Vera Institute of Justice
    b. National Institute of Justice
    c. Los Angeles Probation Department
    d. National Center for State Courts

20. On any given day, there are approximately how many people in the nation's jails?
    a. 100,000
    b. 300,000
    c. 750,000
    d. 1 million

True-False

1. The higher the bail amount, the more likely it is that the accused will be able to post the required bond.
    a. true
    b. false

2.	From the perspective of plea bargaining, pretrial detention and demoralizing jail conditions serve no purpose.
	a.	true
	b.	false

3.	Generally, as jails become overcrowded, bail-setting practices become more severe.
	a.	true
	b.	false

4.	Police can retrieve fugitives with much less legal restrictions than bail bondsmen.
	a.	true
	b.	false

5.	Judges commonly face criticisms mainly for Type 1 errors.
	a.	true
	b.	false

6.	Theoretically, any defendant released on bail could potentially commit another crime.
	a.	true
	b.	false

7.	Defendants charged with murder are the least likely to be denied bail.
	a.	true
	b.	false

8.	The major financial risk that bail bondsmen face is clients who will appear for trial.
	a.	true
	b.	false

9.	Bail bondsmen generally charge a 30% fee based on the bond amount.
	a.	true
	b.	false

10.	Bail bondsmen would commonly consider violent defendants as low risk clients.
	a.	true
	c.	false

11.	The practice of allowing defendants to be released prior to trial originated in England.
	a.	true
	b.	false

12.	Defendants accused of capital offenses commonly have no right to bail.
	a.	true
	b.	false

13. Jailed defendants are less likely to be convicted and sentenced to prison than those on pretrial release.
    a.   true
    b.   false

14. The amount of money paid to the bondsmen by a client is nonrefundable.
    a.   true
    b.   false

15. Prison overcrowding is a major cause of jail overcrowding.
    a.   true
    b.   false

Fill in the Blank

1. Type _____ errors involve releasing a defendant who later commits another crime or fails to appear in court.

2. Bail reform projects are now referred to as pretrial _____ programs.

3. Bounty hunters are also referred to as _____ enforcement agents.

4. Preventative _____ refers to holding suspects accused of committing dangerous or violent crimes in jail to protect the community.

5. The rate of nonappearance decreases as the time from arrest to trial _____.

6. Release on recognizance is the type of bail in which defendants are released if they have strong _____ to the community and are unlikely to flee.

7. Supporters of the _____ model argue that bail should be used to protect society.

8. Another name for a bench warrant is a _____.

9. In some jurisdictions, _____ have replaced the role of bail bondsmen.

10. Type _____ errors involve detaining a suspect who should have been released.

11. Generally, the more serious the crime, the _____ the amount of bail.

12. Trial court judges have virtually unlimited _____ in determining bail.

13. The Bail Reform Act of _____ created a presumption favoring pretrial release.

14. Advocates of pretrial service programs argue that such programs save _____.

15. The higher the bail, the _____ likely it is that the accused will be able to post bond.

Essay

1. Describe the four ways that a defendant may gain pretrial release.

2. What are the three factors that affect pretrial release policies and how do they affect such policies?

3. Explain the reciprocal relationship between the courts and bail bondsmen.

4. Discuss the differences between the approaches towards bail of crime control and due process advocates.

5. What are the two most important factors related to bail setting and how do they effect bail determinations?

CHAPTER 11 ANSWER KEYS

Multiple Choice

1—c	2—a	3—b	4—d	5—c
6—d	7—a	8—c	9—b	10—d
11—b	12—a	13—b	14—a	15—b
16—a	17—d	18—c	19—a	20—c

True-False

1—F	2—F	3—F	4—F	5—T
6—T	7—F	8—F	9—F	10—F
11—T	12—T	13—F	14—T	15—F

Fill in the blank

1—one	2—service	3—bail	4—detention
5—increases	6—ties	7—crime control	8—capias
9—courts	10—two	11—higher	12—discretion
13—1966	14—money	15—less	

Chapter 12
DISCLOSING AND SUPPRESSING EVIDENCE

LEARNING OBJECTIVES

After reading this chapter, students should understand the

- rules of discovery and disclosure of information.
- process reciprocal disclosure between prosecutors and defense attorneys.
- impact of the exclusionary rule.
- various legal views on confessions.
- nature of search and seizure.
- impact of warrant and warrantless searches on criminal cases.
- process of pretrial suppression motions.
- controversy surrounding the exclusionary rule.

CHAPTER OUTLINE

I. **Discovery**
- A. Law on the Books: Rules Requiring Disclosure
  - 1. Civil discovery
    - a. Full disclosure
    - b. Federal Rules of Civil Procedure (1963)
  - 2. Criminal discovery
    - a. No general right to discovery (*Weatherford v. Bursey*)
    - b. Varies greatly from state to state
    - c. Exculpatory evidence must be given to defense (*Brady v. Maryland*)
- B. Law in Action: Informal Prosecutorial Disclosure
  - 1. Disclosure varies between prosecutors' offices.
  - 2. Cooperative defense attorneys often receive more information
    - b. Based on norms of the courtroom work group
  - 3. Informal prosecutorial discovery encourages plea bargains
- C. Law and Controversy: Requiring Reciprocal Disclosure
  - 1. Defense must notify prosecutor of certain defenses (alibi defense)
  - 2. Rights against self-incrimination limit reciprocal discovery

II. **The Exclusionary Rule and the Supreme Court**
- A. Prohibits prosecutors from using illegally obtained evidence
  - 1. A court of law should not participate in nor condone illegal conduct
  - 2. Excluding evidence will deter illegal police behavior
  - 3. Alternative remedies are unworkable

III. **Confessions**
- A. Must be free and voluntary
- B. Court rejected confessions based on coercion

C.   The Warren Court Changes the Rules
    1.   *Miranda* warnings
        a.   Right to remain silent
        b.   Anything you say can be used against you
        c.   Right to an attorney
        c.   Indigents' right to a court appointed attorney
    2.   Shifted burden of proof from defense to prosecutor/police
D.   The Burger and Rehnquist Courts Limit Miranda ruling
    1.   Limited *Miranda* and the exclusionary rule by creating exceptions
        a.   Use of voluntary statements made by defendant
        b.   Public safety exceptions

IV.   Searches and Seizure
A.   Unreasonable searches and seizures
    1.   *Weeks v. U.S.* applied exclusionary rule to federal law enforcement
    2.   *Mapp v. Ohio* applied exclusionary rule to states
    3.   Exclusionary rule limited by creating some exceptions
B.   Search Warrants
    1.   Require probable on oath and signed by a judge
    2.   Rejection of search warrants by judges/magistrates is rare
    3.   Good faith exceptions created by the *Leon* ruling
C.   Warrantless Searches
    1.   Majority of searches conducted without warrants
        a.   Consent
        b.   Search incidental to a lawful arrest
        c.   Plain view

V.   The Exclusionary Rule and the Courtroom Work Group
A.   Pretrial Motions
    1.   Suppression motions must be made prior to trial
    2.   Defense bears the burden of proving search was illegal
B.   Defense Attorney as Prime Mover
    1.   Suppression can lead to a win and discovery of information
    2.   Opens plea bargain options for defense
C.   The Defensive Posture of the Prosecutor
    1.   Suppression motions represent liability
    2.   Prosecutorial power plays a key role
D.   Trial Judges as Decision Makers
    1.   Do not regularly grant suppression motions
E.   Police Testimony
    1.   Police use *Miranda* to cultivate confessions
    2.   3 out of 4 waive their *Miranda* warnings

VI.   Law and Controversy: Costs of the Exclusionary Rule
A.   4.8 percent of all cases are rejected for search and seizure issues
B.   Motions to suppress are filed in less than 8% of all cases

C.   6 of 1000 cases were lost due to exclusionary rules

D.   Majority of lost cases are for drug cases rather than serious crimes

VII.   Conclusion

KEY TERMS

alibi defense - A defense alleging that the defendant was elsewhere at the time of the crime he or she is charged with. (252)

consent search - A person, place, or movables may be lawfully searched by an officer of the law if the owner gives free and voluntary consent. (260)

discovery - Pretrial procedure in which parties to a lawsuit ask for and receive information such as testimony, records, or other evidence from each other. (250)

exclusionary rule - A rule created by judicial decisions holding that evidence obtained through violations of the constitutional rights of the criminal defendant must be excluded from the trial. (253)

illegal search and seizure - An act in violation of the Fourth Amendment of the Constitution. (255)

plain view - If police happen to come across something while acting within their lawful duty, it may be used as evidence in a criminal trial, even if the police did not have a search warrant. (260)

search warrant - A written order, issued by judicial authority, directing a law enforcement officer to search for personal property and, if found, to bring it before the court. (258)

suppression motion - Request that a court of law prohibit specific statements, documents, or objects from being introduced into evidence in a trial. (262)

unreasonable search and seizure - The Fourth Amendment provides for protection against unreasonable searches and seizures, or the illegal gathering of evidence, but was not very effective until the adoption of the exclusionary rule, barring the use of evidence so obtained (*Mapp v. Ohio* 1961). (255)

warrantless search - Search without a search warrant. (260)

CHAPTER SUMMARY

Discovery is the formal and informal exchange of information between the prosecution and defense. Its main purpose of which is to ensure fairness in the adversary system. However, civil and criminal rules for discovery vary greatly. Most civil rules of evidence spawn from the Federal Rules of Civil Procedure (1938). In civil proceedings, every party is entitled to full disclosure, except for privileged information. In contrast, there is no general constitutional right to discovery in criminal proceedings

(*Weatherford b. Bursey*). The type of information that is discoverable varies greatly between the states. However, prosecutors are required to disclose exculpatory evidence (*Brady v. Maryland*).

Policies for disclosure also vary between individual prosecutor's offices. Prosecutors tend to share more information with defense attorneys who are cooperative with the courtroom work group. In general, informal prosecutorial discovery greatly encourages plea bargains. There is also reciprocal disclosure by the defense, in which prosecutors must be notified when using certain defenses or pleas. However, reciprocal discovery is limited because defendants have a 5th Amendment privilege against self-incrimination.

The exclusionary rule prohibits prosecutors from using illegally obtained evidence in court and is the Supreme Court's sole method for enforcing several protected rights. The exclusionary rule has been justified on three grounds. First, a court of law should not participate in nor condone illegal conduct. Second, excluding evidence will deter illegal behavior by police. Third, alternative methods to curb police misconduct have proved unworkable. There are three distinct types of exclusionary rules: identification of suspects, confessions/interrogations, and searches/seizures.

Traditionally, for confessions to be legal, they had to be free and voluntary. In order to better address definitions of coercion, the Court decided the landmark case of *Miranda v. Arizona* in 1966. *Miranda* requires police to inform a suspect of their rights to remain silent and rights to an attorney. Although *Miranda* did not create any new rights for suspects, it greatly changed police practices. *Miranda* also shifted the burden of proof from the defense to prosecutors and police to prove that confessions meet *Miranda* requirements.

The exclusionary rule stands in stark contrast to the common law rule that "if the constable blunders, the crook should not go free." The exclusionary rule regarding searches and seizures was applied to federal law enforcement in *Weeks v. U.S.* and to the states in *Mapp v. Ohio*. There are two types of searches: searches with a warrant and warrantless searches. While often time-consuming, search warrants are rarely rejected by the judge or magistrate. The general rule is that all searches must be conducted with a warrant. However, there are many exceptions and the majority of searches are carried out without a warrant. Some examples would include consent, plain view, and search incident to a lawful arrest. There is also a "Good Faith" exception to the exclusionary rule created by the Court in *U.S. v. Leon*.

While the exclusionary rule is directed at police, the courts enforce it. Most states require that suppression motions be filed prior to a trial. In such hearings, the defense bears the burden of proof and the prosecutor maintains the upper hand. The courtroom work group also plays an important role in influencing the defense attorney's decision to make a motion to suppress. While there is much controversy surrounding the exclusionary rules, scholars point out that they do not have as dire of an impact on the justice system as many would think.

Approximately three out of four suspects waive their *Miranda* rights. The National Institute of Justice found that search and seizure issues account for less than 5% of case rejections. Furthermore, defense attorneys file motions to suppress in less than 8% of all cases and most lost cases are for minor crimes rather than serious crimes. Therefore, some observers would suggest the exclusionary rule perhaps serves to weed out the most blatant cases of police misconduct.

PRACTICE TEST BANK

Multiple Choice

1.   Which of the following is one of the three distinct types of exclusionary rules?
     a.   identification of suspects
     b.   discovery
     c.   suppression
     d.   *Miranda* warnings

2.   Approximately how many suspects waive their *Miranda* warnings?
     a.   1 out of 10
     b.   3 out of 4
     c.   5 out of 10
     d.   1 out of 4

3.   Which of the following Court cases extended the exclusionary rule to the states?
     a.   *Mapp v. Ohio*
     b.   *Terry v. Ohio*
     c.   *Marbury v. Madison*
     d.   *Burns v. Reed*

4.   The National Institute of Justice found that approximately _____ percentage of cases were rejected for search and seizure reasons.
     a.   0.01%
     b.   5%
     c.   25%
     d.   50%

5.   Which Supreme Court case held that police must inform suspects of their rights prior to custodial interrogation?
     a.   *U.S. v. Miller*
     b.   *Texas v. Cobb*
     c.   *Miranda v. Arizona*
     d.   *Mapp v. Ohio*

6.   Which of the following Court decisions created the "good faith" exception to the exclusionary rule?
     a.   *Miranda v. Arizona*
     b.   *Mapp v. Ohio*
     c.   *Terry v. Ohio*
     d.   *U.S. v. Leon*

7.	Which Court decision ruled that the issuance of a speeding ticket does not give police the authority to search the vehicle?
	a.	*Knowles v. Iowa*
	b.	*Chimel v. California*
	c.	*Marbury v. Madison*
	d.	*Texas v. Cobb*

8.	Which Court decision held that the use of physical coercion to obtain confessions violates the due process clause of the 14th Amendment?
	a.	*Miranda v. Arizona*
	b.	*New York v. Quarles*
	c.	*Brown v. Mississippi*
	d.	*Roe v. Wade*

9.	Evidence obtained in illegal searches and seizures may be discarded under the _____.
	a.	First Amendment
	b.	Fourth Amendment
	c.	Fifth Amendment
	d.	Eighth Amendment

10.	The traditional rule regarding confessions is that confessions _____.
	a.	may not be physically coerced
	b.	must be free and voluntary
	c.	may not be psychologically coerced
	d.	may be obtained by any means necessary

11.	The Court ruling in *Brady v. Maryland* applies only to what type of evidence?
	a.	incriminating
	b.	exclamatory
	c.	exculpatory
	d.	confessions

12.	Which of the following are the most likely to involve questions of police conduct?
	a.	burglaries
	b.	DWI cases
	c.	fraud
	d.	weapons and drug cases

13.	Which Amendment to the U.S. Constitution prohibits unreasonable searches and seizures?
	a.	First Amendment
	b.	Second Amendment
	c.	Fourth Amendment
	d.	Sixth Amendment

14. Which of the following Court decisions created the public safety exception to the exclusionary rule?
    a. *Miranda v. Arizona*
    b. *Mapp v. Ohio*
    c. *Roe v. Wade*
    d. *New York v. Quarles*

15. Who commonly maintains the upper hand during pretrial suppression hearings?
    a. police.
    b. prosecutor.
    c. defense attorney.
    d. judge.

16. Which Amendment to the U.S. Constitution provides for protection against self-incrimination?
    a. First Amendment
    b. Fourth Amendment
    c. Fifth Amendment
    d. Eighth Amendment

17. Which Court decision held that once a suspect has invoked his/her right to an attorney, police may not continue interrogation without his/her attorney present?
    a. *Mapp v. Ohio*
    b. *Minnick v. Mississippi*
    c. *Terry v. Ohio*
    d. *Burns v. Reed*

18. Which of the following would likely argue against broader discovery laws?
    a. prosecutors
    b. due process advocates
    c. defense attorneys
    d. defendants

19. Which of the following is incorporated into the *Miranda* warnings?
    a. right to bail
    b. right to an attorney
    c. right to present an alibi
    d. right against cruel and unusual punishment

20. According to Nardulli, motions to suppress evidence are filed in less than what percentage of cases?
    a. 1
    b. 8
    c. 30
    d. 60

True-False

1. During pretrial suppression hearings, the burden of proof lies with the prosecutor.
    a.   true
    b .   false

2. More often than not, judges will reject search warrant affidavits.
    a.   true
    b.   false

3. Police officers are no longer required to advise suspects that they have a right not to consent to a search.
    a.   true
    b.   false

4. Criminal discovery proceedings are generally full disclosure.
    a.   true
    b.   false

5. The *Miranda* decision created new rights for defendants and suspects.
    a.   true
    b.   false

6. The issuance of a speeding ticket gives police the right to search the vehicle.
    a.   true
    b.   false

7. In most states, suppression motions are made during the trial.
    a.   true
    b.   false

8. Defense attorneys often have the upper hand in suppression hearings.
    a.   true
    b.   false

9. The majority of searches by police are conducted without a warrant.
    a.   true
    b.   false

10. Suspects who provide incriminating statements against themselves are more likely to be charged and convicted.
    a.   true
    b.   false

11. The exclusionary rule prohibits prosecutors from using legally obtained evidence in court.
     a.   true
     b.   false

12. Recent conservative courts have strengthened the exclusionary rule.
     a.   true
     b.   false

13. The two types of searches are with and without a warrant.
     a.   true
     b.   false

14. Reasonable suspicion is the primary requirement for a search warrant.
     a.   true
     b.   false

15. Defense attorneys who maintain good relationships with the prosecutor can expect to receive less information than mavericks during discovery.
     a.   true
     b.   false

Fill in the Blank

1.   The exclusionary rule prohibits prosecutors from using illegally obtained _____ in court.

2.   Defense attorneys may file a _____ to suppress evidence that was illegally obtained.

3.   When a police officer informs a suspect of his or her right, this is known as the *Miranda* _____.

4.   _____ discovery refers to the requirement that the defense disclose various materials to the prosecutor prior to trial.

5.   *Weeks v. U.S.* applied the exclusionary rule only to _____ law enforcement.

6.   The Fourth Amendment prohibits _____ searches and seizures.

7.   *Terry v. Ohio* dealt with stop and _____.

8.   While the exclusionary rule is directed at police, it is enforced in _____.

9.   A consent search is a type of _____ search.

10. In *Weatherford v. Bursey*, the Court held that there is no general constitutional right to discovery in a _____ case.

11. In rural areas, a number of search warrants are secured by _____.

12. The decision to suppress evidence rests with the _____.

13. Evidence that shows a defendant's innocence is referred to as _____ evidence.

14. The formal or informal exchange of information between prosecution and defense is referred to as _____.

15. Exculpatory evidence is commonly referred to as _____ material.

Essay

1. Explain the three justifications for the exclusionary rule.

2. What rights and privileges are covered in the *Miranda* warning?

3. List and explain at least three exceptions to the exclusionary rule.

4. In general, what affects have the exclusionary rules and other rules of evidence had on the criminal justice system?

5. Compare and contrast the rules of discovery for criminal and civil proceedings.

CHAPTER 12 ANSWER KEYS

Multiple Choice

1—a	2—b	3—a	4—b	5—c
6—d	7—a	8—c	9—b	10—b
11—c	12—d	13—c	14—d	15—b
16—c	17—b	18—a	19—b	20—b

True-False

1—F	2—F	3—T	4—F	5—F
6—F	7—F	8—F	9—T	10—T
11—T	12—F	13—T	14—F	15—F

Fill in the blank

1—evidence	2—motion	3—warning	4—Reciprocal
5—federal	6—unreasonable	7—frisk	8—courts
9—warrantless	10—criminal	11—telephone	12—judge
13—exculpatory	14—discovery	15—*Brady*	

Chapter 13
NEGOTIATED JUSTICE AND THE PLEA OF GUILTY

LEARNING OBJECTIVES

After reading this chapter, students should understand the
- various types of plea agreements.
- relationship between caseloads and plea bargaining.
- factors of discretion and negotiated justice.
- courtroom work group's impact on plea bargains.
- underlying dynamics of plea bargains.
- process of defendants who enter a plea of guilty.
- implications of abolishing plea bargaining.
- nature of reforming plea bargains.

CHAPTER OUTLINE

I. **Law on the Books: Types of Plea Agreements**
   A. Plea bargaining involves the prosecutor offering some gain to the defendant in return for the defendant pleading guilty
      1. Charge bargaining
      2. Count bargaining
      3. Sentence bargaining

II. **Law in Action: Bargaining and Caseloads**
   A. The excessive caseload hypothesis suggests it is in response to a need to move cases quickly
   B. Workgroup members have discretion and common interest in not spending trying cases about which there are no significant legal or factual issues

III. **Law in Action: Bargaining and Discretion**
   A. Presumption of Factual Guilt
   B. Costs and Risks of Trial
   C. What to do with the Guilty

IV. **Bargaining and the Courtroom Work Group**
   A. Prosecutors
      1. Certainty of conviction
      2. Controls the negotiating process
   B. Defendants
      1. Possibility of a lenient sentence
      2. Must formally waive rights and receive an explanation
   C. Defense Attorneys
      1. Assesses the offer in the best interest of their client
   D. Judges
      1. Few are actively involved in plea negotiations

V.   Dynamics of Bargaining
  A.   Decision-Making Norms
    1.   Seriousness of the crime
    2.   Prior criminal record
    3.   Strength of the prosecutor's case
  B.   Why Cases Go to Trial
    1.   Chance of acquittal
    2.   Prison sentence is high
    3.   Irrational defendants
  C.   Jury Trial Penalty
    1.   Notion of being more severe for taking the time of the court

VI.   Copping a Plea
  A.   Questioning the Defendant
    1.   *Nolo contendere* pleas (no contest)
    2.   Guilty
      a.   Courts generally require defendant's to read and sign a form (Boykin form)
  B.   Accepting a Plea
    1.   Judges have discretion to reject plea of guilty
    2.   Acceptance of *Alford* pleas (guilty while innocent)
  C.   Placing the Plea Agreement on the Record
    1.   Plea must be on the record
    2.   Limited right to withdraw a guilty plea

VII.   Law in Controversy: Abolishing Plea Bargaining
  A.   Are the Changes Implemented?
    1.   Plea bargaining contributes to the efficiency of the process
    2.   Attempts to abolish bargaining have seemingly failed to produce results
  B.   Is Discretion Eliminated or Just Moved Elsewhere?
    1.   California's Proposition 8 relocated plea bargaining to lower court
    2.   Alaska's attempt to abolish reemerged as charge bargaining
  C.   Do Offsetting Changes Occur?
    1.   Dismissals might increase as demand for trials increase
    2.   More offenders sentenced as juveniles rather than adults
    3.   Attempts to abolish plea bargains often fail to consider the reasons for plea negotiations, which leads to their failure

VIII.   Conclusion

KEY TERMS

Boykin form - Document intended to show that the defendant entered a guilty plea voluntarily and intelligently, understanding the charges and consequences of conviction (*Boykin v.Alabama*, 1969). (281)

charge bargaining - In return for the defendant's plea of guilty, the prosecutor allows the defendant to plead guilty to a less serious charge than the one originally filed. (272)

count bargaining - The defendant pleads guilty to some, but not all, of the counts contained in the charging document, which reduces the potential sentence. (273)

nolo contendere - Latin phrase meaning "I will not contest it." A plea of "no contest" in a criminal case means that the defendant does not directly admit guilt but submits to sentencing or other punishment. (281)

plea bargaining - The process by which a defendant pleads guilty to a criminal charge with the expectation of receiving some benefit from the state. (272)

plea on the nose - The defendant pleads guilty to the charges contained in the indictment or bill of information. (274)

sentence bargaining - The defendant pleads guilty knowing the sentence that will be imposed; the sentence in the sentence bargain is less than the maximum. (274)

CHAPTER SUMMARY

Plea bargaining vividly illustrates the difference between law on the books and law in action. It also illustrates the difference between the public conception and the reality. The rules of criminal procedure, decisions of appellate courts, theories of the adversary system, and the media all suggest that the trial is the principal activity of the criminal courts. Instead, plea bargaining is the dominant activity.

Bargaining is best understood not as a response to large caseloads (caseload hypothesis) but as an adaptation to the realities of the types of cases requiring disposition. In most cases, there is little question about the defendant's legal guilt. A trial is a costly and sometimes risky method of establishing that guilt, and it cannot wrestle with the pressing issue of what sentence to impose. Through plea bargaining, courthouse officials are able to individualize justice. In many instances, it is neither necessary nor desirable that every defendant has a trial.

There is evidence that plea bargaining became a common practice in state courts sometime after the Civil War. In federal courts, the massive number of cases stemming from Prohibition led to the institutionalization of plea bargaining in the first third of the twentieth century. What is new is the controversy over it and the amount of attention plea negotiations now receive.

In most cases, the defendant's interest in plea bargaining is to obtain the most lenient sentence possible. Plea bargaining generally takes 3 forms: charge bargaining, count bargaining, and/or sentence bargaining. In charge bargaining, in return for the defendant's plea of guilty, the prosecutor allows the defendant to plead guilty to a less serious charge than the one originally filed. For example, the defendant pleads guilty to misdemeanor assault rather than the original charge of aggravated assault, a felony. The principal effect of a plea to a less serious charge is to reduce the potential sentence. Some offenses carry a high maximum sentence. A plea to a lesser charge therefore greatly reduces the possible prison term the defendant might have to serve. Bargains for reduced charges are most commonly found in jurisdictions where the state's criminal code is severe and/or where prosecutors, routinely overcharge. Thus, some charge reductions reflect the possibility that the prosecutor would not be able to convict for the original charge at trial. The second common type of plea agreement is called count bargaining. In return for the defendant's plea of guilty to one or more counts in the indictment or information, the prosecutor dismisses the remaining counts. For example, a defendant accused of three separate robberies pleads guilty to one robbery count, and the two remaining criminal charges are dismissed. Like a charge reduction agreement, a count bargain reduces the defendant's potential sentence. The third type of bargaining is sentence bargaining. The defendant agrees to plead guilty in return for the prosecution recommending a particular sentence.

The common explanation for plea bargaining is that the courts have too many cases. It was argued that although this explanation contains some truth, it obscures too many important facets of what the courts do and why they do it. But the caseload hypothesis cannot explain why plea bargaining is as prevalent in courts with relatively few cases as it is in courts with heavy caseloads.

The possibility of trial greatly influences negotiations and the courtroom workgroup. Trials are a costly and time-consuming means of establishing guilt. Yet, most cases do not have significant factual or legal issues. Most of the weak cases have already been weeded out. The workgroups has developed norms about normal cases and normal sentences. Based on these considerations, all members of the courtroom work group have a common interest in disposing of cases and avoiding unnecessary trials.

There are certain legal formalities that are supposed to be observed in entering a guilty plea. There must be waivers of the rights the defendant is giving up. Further, both the defendant and government have an obligation to keep the bargain. If not, the plea may be withdrawn or cancelled. Although the U.S. Supreme Court has heard a number of cases on this topic, it has generally supported plea bargaining.

PRACTICE TEST BANK

Multiple Choice

1. A _____ plea has the same criminal court consequences as a *nolo contendere* plea.
    a. guilty
    b. not guilty
    c. not guilty by reason of insanity
    d. prior jeopardy

2. A defendant pleading guilty is generally required to read and sign a _____ form.
    a. Santobello
    b. Reeves
    c. Jones
    d. Boykin

3. A/n _____ plea is one in which the defendant pleads guilty but maintains innocence.
    a. Crockett
    b. Alford
    c. Santobello
    d. Ruiz

4. Due _____ model advocates and liberals criticize plea bargaining because they fear that defendants are unfairly denied their rights.
    a. regard
    b. substance
    c. process
    d. deference

5. Plea bargaining seems to be contrary to the concept of an _____ system of justice.
    a. adversary
    b. free will
    c. inquisitorial
    d. impartial

6. A defendant is charged with armed or aggravated robbery. The prosecutor will accept a plea to regular (unarmed) robbery. This is an example of a _____ bargain.
    a. charge
    b. sentence
    c. count
    d. sanction

7. The main difference between a guilty plea and a *nolo contendere* plea is that the guilty plea _____.
   a. can be used in a civil proceeding against the defendant
   b. results only in a conditional conviction
   c. cannot be withdrawn later under any circumstances
   d. can be used in a civil proceeding against the defendant as an admission of liability

8. Prosecutors sometimes _____ to gain a potential advantage in later plea bargaining.
   a. demand grand jury review
   b. intentionally overcharge
   c. waive a preliminary hearing
   d. file habeas corpus

9. In a plea _____, the defendant pleads to the original charge.
   a. of prior jeopardy
   b. of *non compos mentos*
   c. on the nose
   d. *pro forma*

10. Crime_____ model advocates, conservatives and crime victims criticize plea bargaining because they fear that the sentences will be too lenient.
    a. adversary
    b. abatement
    c. process
    d. control

11. If the defendant wants to enter an _____ plea, the judge can accept it only if there is substantial evidence of guilt.
    a. *nolo contendere*
    b. Ruiz
    c. Bordenkircher
    d. Alford

12. Plea bargaining first became commonplace in state courts shortly after the _____ War.
    a. Spanish-American
    b. Revolutionary
    c. Mexican
    d. Civil

13. Which of the following is not one of the three common types of plea bargaining?
    a. charge
    b. count
    c. disposition
    d. sentence

14. Everyone in the courtroom workgroup has an interest in _____.
    a. getting new clients
    b. avoiding unnecessary trials
    c. appearing tough on crime
    d. getting re-elected

15. As compared to more serious charges, defendants charged with less serious crimes such as DWI or theft are _____.
    a. more likely to accept a plea bargain
    b. more likely to go to trial
    c. less likely to go to trial
    d. more likely to get a dismissal during trial

16. In federal courts, plea bargaining first became prominent in/during _____.
    a. Prohibition
    b. the depression of 1917
    c. the Viet Nam war era
    d. the Ford administration

17. When a case reaches the trial stage, the defendant is tagged with a presumption of factual guilt because _____.
    a. most defendants cannot afford a private attorney
    b. the judge has weeded out the charges against innocent persons
    c. the prosecution has plead out or dismissed the weak cases
    d. most defendants are poor and uneducated

18. A defendant who is clearly guilty but demands a jury trial _____.
    a. is still likely to be acquitted
    b. may suffer the jury trial penalty
    c. will have to obtain a private attorney even if indigent
    d. will get into court quicker than one who wants to plead guilty

19. In federal courts, and most, if not all, jurisdictions, the terms of the plea bargain _____.
    a. must be approved by the victim
    b. must be read into the record
    c. must be submitted to the judge at least seven days in advance
    d. are not binding if no consideration has changed hands

20. A defendant's guilty plea must be _____.
    a. inculpatory, cognate and sensate
    b. exculpatory, and cognitive and volitional
    c. volitional, exculpatory and perfidious
    d. knowing, intelligent and voluntary

True-False

1. Overall, the seriousness of the offense is the not an important factor in how the courtroom workgroup approaches plea negotiations.
    a.   true
    b.   false

2. There is mixed research both supporting and denying the existence of a jury trial penalty.
    a.   true
    b.   false

3   A *nolo contendere* plea involves a waiver of a number of important rights.
    a.   true
    b.   false

4. A *nolo contendere* plea has all the same criminal and civil consequences as a guilty plea.
    a.   true
    b.   false

5. An *Alford* plea is commonly used as a form of sentence bargaining.
    a.   true
    b.   false

6. Supporters of the crime control model worry that plea bargaining negates the protections of the adversary system.
    a.   true
    b.   false

7. Plea bargaining did not become well established in the U.S. until the 1940s.
    a   true
    b.   false

8. Murder, rape and robbery defendants are more likely to plead guilty than those charged with lesser crimes.
    a.   true
    b.   false

9. After dismissing weak cases, the defense attorney proceeds from a position of strength in plea bargaining.
    a.   true
    b.   false

10. The Burger Court refused to ban plea bargaining.
    a.   true
    b.   false

11. The 1973 National Advisory Commission on Criminal Justice Standards and Goals recommended that plea bargaining be limited to misdemeanors and non-violent felonies.
   a. true
   b. false

12. More cases are disposed of by dismissals and pleas than by trials.
   a. true
   b. false

13. The judge usually knows less about each case than the prosecutor and defense attorney.
   a. true
   b. false

14. If either side violates the terms of a plea bargain, the only remedy is in a civil court.
   a. true
   b. false

15. A *nolo contendere* plea is the same as an acquittal.
   a. true
   b. false

Fill in the Blank

1. The term "plea on the nose" means the defendants pleads guilty to the _____ original charge.

2. A plea of _____ is the criminal equivalent of a guilty plea.

3. In *Ricketts v.* _____ (1987) the U.S. Supreme Court held that defendants must live up to their side of the plea bargain or face the consequences of trial.

4. Attempts to outlaw plea bargaining occurred in _____, Michigan and Alaska.

5. In *Bordenkircher v.* _____ (1978) the U.S. Supreme Court validated a plea bargain even though the prosecutor threatened to bring additional lawful charges against the defendant if the defendant refused to plead guilty.

6. A *nolo contendere* or guilty plea involves a _____ of many constitutional rights.

7. Bargaining about which charge in the indictment the defendant will plead to is called _____ bargaining.

8. Defendants may be required to read and sign _____ forms before pleading guilty.

9. A/n _____ plea is one at which the defendant pleads guilty but still maintains innocence.

10. Shortly after the _____ War, plea bargaining became common in state courts.

11. _____ process model adherents criticize plea bargaining because they fear defendants will railroaded and denied their rights.

12 The theory of _____ processes posits that changes at one stage or in one part of the system will sometimes be cancelled out by changes at another stage or part of the system.

13. In *Santobello v. N.Y.*, the U.S. Supreme Court held that _____ must keep their side of the plea bargain.

14. During _____ plea bargaining became commonplace in federal courts.

15. Those who support the crime _____ model worry that plea bargaining results in excessively lenient sentences.

Essay

1. Discuss some of the explanations for the existence of plea bargaining. Which do you think is the best explanation?

2. Compare and contrast the due process and crime control model evaluations of plea bargaining. Which model do you find most convincing on this issue? Be sure to explain your position.

3. Compare and contrast count, sentencing and charge plea bargains. Be sure to provide examples.

4. Discuss the pros and cons of abolishing plea bargaining. What is your position on the issue? Be sure to explain your position and provide examples.

5. Discuss and explain the hydraulic effects theory of what happens when a jurisdiction abolishes or severely limits plea bargaining. Be sure to provide examples.

CHAPTER 13 ANSWER KEYS

Multiple Choice

1—a	2—d	3—b	4—c	5—a
6—a	7—a	8—b	9—c	10—d
11—d	12—d	13—c	14—b	15—a
16—a	17—c	18—b	19—b	20—d

True-False

1—F	2—T	3—T	4—F	5—F
6—F	7—F	8—F	9—F	10—T
11—F	12—T	13—T	14—F	15—F

Fill in the blank

1—original	2—nolo contendere	3—Adamson	4—California
5—Hayes	6—waiver	7—count	8—Boykin
9—Alford	10—Civil	11—due	12—hydraulic
13—prosecutors	14—Prohibition	15—control	

Chapter 14
TRIALS AND JURIES

After reading this chapter, students should understand the

- history of using trials by jury.
- basic features of trial juries.
- process for selecting trial juries.
- *voir dire* process and the role of jury consultants.
- various stages of the prosecutorial trail process.
- role and function of the defense in a jury trial.
- nature of jury instructions and deliberations.
- various factors affecting jury verdicts.

CHAPTER OUTLINE

I. **History of Trial by Jury**
    A. Juries prevent oppression by government and overzealous prosecutors
    B. English Roots
        1. The first juries were used in ancient Greece, Rome, and France
        2. The English Magna Carta in 1215 recognized a right to a jury trial
    C. Colonial Developments
        1. Jury trials mentioned in U.S. Constitution.

II. **Law on the Books: The Constitution and Trial by Jury**
    A. Sixth Amendment right to jury trial applies state and federal courts
    B. Scope of the Right to a Trial by Jury
        1. Varies state-to-state. Sixth Amendment applies only to serious offenses
    C. Jury Size
        1. Not all juries require 12 jurors. Florida uses 6 member juries
    D. Unanimity
        1. Five states do not require unanimous verdicts.

III. **Law on the Books: Selecting a Fair and Unbiased Jury**
    A. Master Jury List
        1. Potential jurors selected randomly from master list (often voter registration lists)
    B. Venire
        1. Some jurors excused due to statutory exemptions
    C. *Voir Dire*
        1. Challenges for cause decided by a judge
        2. Peremptory challenge is exclusion without giving a reason
    D. Jury Duty
        1. Most jurors take their duty seriously

IV. **Law in Action: Choosing a Jury Biased in Your Favor**
  A.   Educating Jurors
     1.   Using *Voir Dire* to eliminate bias
  B.   Jury Consultants
     1.   Most hired by defense attorneys
     2.   No convincing evidence that consultant's work is scientific

V. **Overview of a Trial**
  A.   Opening statements

VI. **The Prosecution Presents its Case**
  A.   Burden of Proof
     1.   Defendant has presumption of innocence
     2.   Prosecution must prove guilt beyond reasonable doubt
  B.   Types of Evidence
     1.   Evidence is classified into:
        a.   Real evidence
        b.   Direct evidence
        c.   Circumstantial evidence
  C.   Rules of Evidence: Trustworthiness
     1.   Both sides present evidence but are limited by rules of evidence that attempt to exclude evidence that is not trustworthy
     2.   Hearsay is secondhand evidence
  D.   Rules of Evidence: Relevance
     1.   Valid evidence is termed immaterial or irrelevant
  E.   Scientific Evidence
     1.   Frye test and Daubert doctrine
  F.   Objections to the Admission of Evidence
     1.   Each side can object to admission of the other side's evidence and cross-examine the other side's witnesses

VII. **The Defense Presents its Case**
  A.   Reasonable Doubt
     1.   Skillful use of the right to confront witnesses
  B.   The Defendant as Witness
     1.   The Fifth Amendment gives the defendant a privilege not to testify
  C.   Alibi Defense
     1.   Each side has an opportunity to present rebuttal evidence that challenges the opponent's evidence
  D.   Affirmative Defenses
     1.   Legal excuses such as self-defense, duress, or entrapment
  E.   Challenging Scientific Evidence

VIII. **Rebuttal**
  A.   Discredits the testimony of a previous witness

IX. **Closing Arguments**
  A. Case summations by both prosecutor and defense
  B. Often the most dramatic stage of a trial

X. **Jury Instructions**
  A. Judge instructs jury on law relevant to case following a charging conference

XI. **Jury Deliberations**
  A. What Motivates a Jury?
    1. 90 percent of the majority vote will win out after the first ballot
  B. Are Juries Biases?
    1. Overall, jurors appear to be fair and impartial

XII. **The Verdict**
  A. Jurors convict in 82% of federal cases and around two-thirds of state cases

XIII. **Post-Verdict Motions**
  A. Acquittal (not guilty)
  B. Motion for a new trial most common (few are ever granted)

XIV. **Law in Action: Trials as Balancing Wheels**
  A. Popular Standards of Justice
    1. Jury nullification (refusal of jury to apply the law)
  B. Uncertainty
    1. Irrational decisions by juries

XV. **Prejudicial Pretrial Publicity**
  A. Pretrial publicity can make obtaining an impartial jury and fair trial difficult
  B. Public and media have First Amendment rights that must be balanced against defendant's right to fair trial
  C. Limited Gag Order
    1. Order prohibiting those involved from providing information to media
  D. Change of Venue
    1. Move trial to another location
  E. Sequestering the Jury
    1. Isolate the jury and keep them together

XVI. **Conclusion**

KEY TERMS

acquittal - The decision of the judge or jury that the defendant is not guilty. (309)

affirmative defense - Without denying the charge, defendant raises extenuating or mitigating circumstances, such as insanity, self-defense, or entrapment. (305)

alibi defense - A defense alleging that the defendant was elsewhere at the time of the crime he or she is charged with. (304)

alternate jurors - Jurors chosen in excess of the minimum number needed, in case one or more jurors is unable to serve for the entire trial. (301)

bench trial - Trial before a judge without a jury. (293)

best-evidence rule - Rule requiring that someone coming into court must bring the best available original evidence to prove the questions involved in the case. (302)

burden of proof - The requirement to introduce evidence to prove an alleged fact or set of facts. (301)

challenge for cause - Method for excusing a potential juror because of specific reasons such as bias or prejudgment; can be granted only by the judge. (297)

change of venue - The removal of a case from one jurisdiction to another. It is usually granted if the court believes that, due to prejudice, a defendant cannot receive a fair trial in the area where the crime occurred. (312)

charging conference - Meeting attended by judge, prosecutor, and defense attorney during which the judge's instructions to the jury are discussed. (307)

circumstantial evidence - An indirect method of proving the material facts of a case; testimony that is not based on the witness's personal observation of the material events. (301)

closing argument - Statement made by an attorney at the end of the presentation of evidence in which the attorney summarizes the case for the jury. (307)

contempt of court - The failure or refusal to obey a court order; may be punished by a fine or imprisonment. (312)

cross-examination - At trial, the questions of one attorney put to a witness called by the opposing attorney. (303)

direct evidence - Evidence derived from one or more of the five senses. (301)

duress - Unlawful pressure on a person to do what he or she would not otherwise have done. (305)

entrapment - The act of a government official or agent inducing a person to commit a crime that the person would not have committed without the inducement. (305)

evidence - Any kind of proof offered to establish the existence or nonexistence of a fact in dispute— for example, testimony, writings, other material objects, demonstrations. (301)

gag order - A judge's order that lawyers and witnesses not discuss the trial with outsiders. (314)

hearsay - An out-of-court assertion or statement, made by someone other than the testifying witness, which is offered to prove the truth of testimony. Hearsay evidence is excluded from trials unless it falls within one of the recognized exceptions. (302)

hung jury - A jury that is unable to reach a verdict. (308)

immaterial - Evidence that neither proves nor disproves the issue of a trial. (302)

impeach - To question the truthfulness of a witness's testimony. (302)

irrelevant - Testimony that has no bearing on the issue of a trial. (302)

jury deliberations - The action of a jury in determining the guilt or innocence, or sentence, of a defendant. (308)

jury instructions - Directions given by a judge to the members of the jury informing them of the law applicable to the case. (307)

jury nullification - Idea that juries have the right to refuse to apply the law in criminal cases despite facts that leave no reasonable doubt that the law was violated. (311)

master jury list - A list of potential jurors in a court's district, from which a representative cross section of the community in which a crime allegedly was committed can be selected for a trial. It is usually compiled from multiple sources, such as voter registration lists, driver's license lists, utility customer lists, and telephone directories. Also called *jury wheel* or *master wheel*. (296)

mistrial - Invalid trial. (303)

objection - The act of taking exception to a statement or procedure during a trial. (303)

CHAPTER SUMMARY

Trials attract more publicity than any other part of the judicial process. Trials are central to the entire scheme of Anglo-American law. Trials provide the ultimate forum for vindicating either the defendant or prosecution. The right to be tried by a jury is guaranteed in several places in the Constitution. The primary purpose of the jury is to prevent oppression by the government and provide the accused protection against the corrupt or overzealous prosecutor and against the compliant, biased, or eccentric judge.

Juries have a long history in the western world. They were first used in Athens five or six centuries B.C. They were later employed by the Romans. They reappeared in France during the ninth century and were later transferred to England. The concept of the jury functioning as an impartial fact-finding body was first formalized in the Magna Carta of 1215, when English noblemen forced the king to recognize limits on his power.

Trials are relatively infrequent events. Roughly 95 percent of all felony convictions result from guilty pleas. However, each year, 2 million jurors serve in some 200,000 civil and criminal cases. Although, only a relative smattering of cases are ever tried the possibility of trial shapes the entire process.

The Sixth Amendment applies in both state and federal courts. However, the right to a jury trial applies only when the offense is a serious or non-petty one (possible incarceration of more than six months). The Sixth Amendment does not require unanimous verdicts or twelve person juries.

The process of ultimately selecting a jury begins with randomly drawing persons from the master jury list. These persons will be summoned to the courthouse. Not all of those summoned will appear, and not all of those who appear will be selected for jury duty. Some categories of persons (e.g., doctors, public school teachers) can claim exemption from service.

The potential jurors will be questioned about their knowledge of the case, ability to be fair, etc. This process is called *voir dire*. During *voir dire*, both attorneys will attempt to educate the jury on points favorable to their side. Potential jurors who cannot be fair can be stricken by challenges for cause. In addition, both sides have a limited number of peremptory challenges that can be used to eliminate potential jurors without providing a reason. Only impartial persons are supposed to be on the jury, but pretrial publicity can make finding an impartial jury difficult. The judge may order a change of venue, moving the trial to another city or county because of excessive local publicity. A judge may issue a gag order prohibiting persons involved from providing information to the media.

After the jury has been selected, the attorneys will make their opening statements where they preview their evidence and legal arguments. The prosecution presents its evidence first because it has the burden of proof. The prosecution must prove the defendant guilty beyond a reasonable doubt. After the prosecution presents its evidence the defense will have an opportunity to present evidence, including defenses such as entrapment, self-defense, duress, etc. Each side will also have an opportunity to present rebuttal evidence to answer the opponent's evidence.

Both sides will present evidence to try to convince the jury. Most of the evidence is testimony of witnesses. Real (physical) or documentary evidence may also be presented. The admissibility of evidence is limited by the rules of evidence that attempt to exclude evidence that is not trustworthy or reliable.

During the trial, attorneys will attempt to block their opponent's evidence by objecting to its admissibility. The judge determines the admissibility of evidence.

Witnesses will be subjected to cross-examination by the opponent of the party that called them. The Sixth Amendment gives defendants the right to confront opposing witnesses.

The Fifth Amendment privilege against self-incrimination gives the defendant a right not to testify if he or she so decides. However, a defendant who testifies can be cross-examined like any other witness.

After all the evidence has been received, the attorneys make their closing arguments. Each side will attempt to persuade the jury to return a verdict in its favor. The judge will then instruct the jury on the law relevant to the case. Juries will sometimes engage in jury nullification, which means that they ignore the law and acquit an obviously guilty defendant.

The jury then deliberates in private. If they cannot reach a verdict, this is termed a hung jury and the defendant may be tried again. If there is a possibility that the jury may be influenced by the media or other events, the jury may be sequestered (kept together and isolated from contact). Although there are occasional highly questionable jury verdicts and some evidence that juries consider improper factors, overall juries appear to perform fairly and base their verdicts on legal factors.

If the defendant is found guilty, he or she will be sentenced. However, defendants can file post-trial motions to try to get the verdict overturned.

PRACTICE TEST BANK

Multiple Choice

1. Jury nullification occurs when a jury _____.
    a.   ignores the law and acquits an obviously guilty defendant
    b.   is unable to reach a verdict
    c.   asks the judge to declare a mistrial
    d.   refuses to deliberate

2. Perhaps the best-known example of _____violating a defendant's right to a fair trial was the murder conviction of Dr. Sam Sheppard.
    a.   bias in jury selection
    b.   prejudicial pretrial publicity
    c.   jury tampering
    d.   a judge's wrongful refusal to grant peremptory challenges

3. The term change of _____ refers to changing the place (city or county) where the trial will be held.
    a.   jurisdiction
    b.   venue
    c.   sequestration
    d.   comity

4. In England, the concept of a jury functioning as an impartial fact-finding body was first formalized in _____ in the Magna Carta.
    a.   1160
    b.   1215
    c.   1492
    d.   1502

5. A constitutional right to jury trial is found in the _____ Amendment.
    a.   Third
    b.   Fifth
    c.   Sixth
    d.   Eighth

6. Under the Sixth Amendment, a defendant has a right to a jury trial only if the offense is punishable by _____.
    a.   death
    b.   life sentence or death
    c.   more than 6 months imprisonment
    d.   any form of incarceration

7. Challenges _____ require an attorney to give a reason why the potential juror should be removed from the jury pool.
   a. for cause
   b. because of a statutory exemption
   c. by reason
   d. *de jure*

8. _____ is the questioning of potential jurors.
   a. Veneration
   b. Vexation
   c. *Vox populi*
   d. *Voir dire*

9. Attorneys do not have to give a reason for exercising their _____ challenges to potential jurors.
   a. mandatory
   b. peremptory
   c. discretionary
   d. preemptive

10. Defense attorneys frequently use _____ to educate jurors about the presumption of innocence and the defense theory of the case
    a. subliminal messages
    b. challenges
    c. objections
    d. *voir dire*

11 Under the _____ rule, only the original of a document is admissible into evidence.
   a. hearsay
   b. judicial notice
   c. best-evidence
   d. privileged communication

12. A hung jury is one which _____.
    a. is unwilling to follow the judge's instructions
    b. acquits an obviously guilty person
    d. cannot agree on a foreperson
    d. is unable to reach a verdict

13. Which of the following is most likely to be hearsay testimony?
    a. "As best I can recall . . ."
    b. "Mary told me that she saw . . ."
    c. "I told my wife . . ."
    d. "I don't remember hearing anyone say . . ."

14. A/n _____ trial is one before a judge without a jury.
    a   bench
    b.   judge
    c.   justice
    d.   abbreviated

15. Questioning of a witness called by the opposing party is termed _____.
    a.   direct examination
    b.   cross-examination
    c.   impeaching interrogation
    d.   collateral questioning

16. If a judge declares a mistrial, this means that _____.
    a.   the trial will be terminated
    b.   the judge finds the defendant not guilty
    c.   a continuance has been granted
    d.   the judge is dismissing the charge

17. The _____ Amendment gives a criminal defendant the right to confront and cross-examine prosecution witnesses.
    a.   Fifth
    b.   Sixth
    c.   Seventh
    d.   Eighth

18. The _____ Amendment gives a criminal defendant a privilege not to testify at trial.
    a.   Fourth
    b.   Fifth
    c.   Sixth
    d.   Eighth
    d.   Thirteenth

19. The judge explains the relevant law to the jury charging the jury or giving _____.
    a.   instructions
    b.   *voir dire*
    c.   verdict form
    d.   elucidation

20. If a case gets to a jury trial, the odds are that _____.
    a.   the defendant will be acquitted
    b.   the defendant will be convicted
    c.   there will be a hung jury
    d.   the judge will declare a mistrial

True-False

1. The idea of jury trials originally came from ancient Greece.
    a.   true
    b.   false

2. A petit jury is considered the same as a trial jury.
    a.   true
    b.   false

3. Article III, section 2 of the Constitution includes the right of a jury trial.
    a.   true
    b.   false

4. The general rule is that hearsay evidence is admissible.
    a.   true
    b.   false

5. Real evidence consists of the testimony of witnesses.
    a.   true
    b.   false

6. The Sixth Amendment gives defendants the right to confront the witnesses against them.
    a.   true
    b.   false

7. Most states have retained the insanity defense.
    a.   true
    b.   false

8. Under the Sixth Amendment, all persons charged with a misdemeanor for which imprisonment is authorized, have a right to a jury trial.
    a.   true
    b.   false

9. The Sixth Amendment does not require that all state criminal jury trials contain twelve persons.
    a.   true
    b.   false

10. The U.S. Supreme Court has approved criminal jury verdicts on a 4-1 vote.
    a.   true
    b.   false

11   Surveys reveal that most citizens express great dissatisfaction overall with jury duty.
        a.   true
        b.   false

12.   Defendants who testify can be cross-examined.
        a.   true
        b.   false

13.   Rebuttal evidence is offered by a party to challenge evidence offered by the opponent.
        a.   true
        b.   false

14.   The venire is the jury plus any alternatives selected to hear a case.
        a.   true
        b.   false

15.   An acquittal is a verdict of not guilty.
        a.   true
        b.   false

Fill in the Blank

1.   A petit jury is also called a _____ jury.

2.   The prejudicial effects of pretrial publicity can sometimes be overcome by a
        _____ of venue.

3.   Article Three section _____ of the Constitution contains a right to a jury trial.

4.   A _____ trial is one before a judge without a jury.

5.   A _____ challenge to a potential juror is one an attorney can use without
        providing a justification.

6.   Jury_____ is the power of a jury to ignore the law.

7.   A _____ jury is one that is unable to reach a verdict.

8.   A/n _____ is the means by which an attorney challenges the admissibility of an
        opponent's evidence.

9.   At least for non-capital cases, the smallest jury thus far approved by the Supreme Court
        is_____ persons

10.   _____ evidence is that which attempts to prove a fact by inference (indirectly).

11.	If a potential juror cannot lay aside their prejudice or bias, an attorney can have them removed or stricken by use of a challenge for _____ .

12.	The _____ entrapment defense involves unacceptable police conduct that induces people to commit crimes.

13.	Eyewitness testimony is an example of _____ evidence.

14.	Backup jurors who may serve if a regular juror is unable to continue are called _____ jurors.

15.	A _____ order is a court order prohibiting persons involved in the case from giving information to the media.

Essay

1.	Discuss fully the current status of the Sixth Amendment right to a jury trial.

2.	Define and discuss jury nullification. Be sure to provide an example. Should a jury be told that they have such a right? Be sure to explain your position.

3.	Discuss the general steps in selecting a jury from creation of the master list to selection of the jurors who will hear the case. Be sure to provide examples.

4.	Discuss the results of some of the research on juries. Does this research reflect favorably or unfavorably on juries as fair decision makers? Be sure to explain your position.

5.	Discuss the history of the jury trial up to and including the Bill of Rights.

CHAPTER 14 ANSWER KEYS

<u>Multiple Choice</u>

1—a	2—b	3—b	4—b	5—c
6—c	7—a	8—d	9—b	10—d
11—c	12—d	13—c	14—a	15—b
16—a	17—b	18—b	19—a	20—b

<u>True-False</u>

1—T	2—T	3—T	4—F	5—F
6—T	7—T	8—F	9—T	10—F
11—F	12—T	13—T	14—F	15—T

<u>Fill in the blank</u>

1—trial	2—change	3—Two	4—bench
5—peremptory	6—nullification	7—hung	8—objection
9—six	10—Circumstantial	11—cause	12—entrapment
13—direct	14—alternate	15—gag	

Chapter 15
SENTENCING OPTIONS

LEARNING OBJECTIVES

After reading this chapter, student should understand the

- nature and extent of sentencing for criminal offenses.
- concepts of deterrence and rehabilitation.
- legal responsibility for sentencing.
- nature and effectiveness of imprisonment.
- effectiveness of probation sentences.
- frequency and effectiveness of using fines and restitution for sanctions.
- various forms of intermediate sanctions.
- nature and effectiveness of using the death penalty for punishment.

CHAPTER OUTLINE

I. **Why Do We Sentence?**
  A. Retribution
    1. Oldest theory
    2. Eye for an eye
    3. Modern just deserts theory is similar—criminals deserve to be punished
  B. Incapacitation
    1. Crime is prevented by physically constraining offenders
    2. Selective incapacitation focuses on small number of multiple offenders
  C. Deterrence
    1. Threat of punishment will keep people from crime
    2. Assumes rational and calculating behavior
  D. Rehabilitation
    1. Treatment programs will turn offender into law abiding citizens
    2. Many question whether rehabilitation programs can work
  E. Competing Sentencing Philosophies

II. **Who Should Decide the Sentence?**
  A. Legislative Sentencing Responsibility
    1. Indeterminate and determinate sentencing
  B. Judicial Sentencing Responsibility
    1. Judges impose sentences within range prescribed by legislature
  C. Executive Sentencing Responsibility
    1. Parole and length of stay in prison
    2. Issuance of "good time" and pardons

III. **What Sentence Should be Imposed?**
  A. Issue of cruel and unusual punishment

IV.   **Imprisonment**
  A.   The United States imprisons its population more than any other nation
  B.   Prison Overcrowding
    1.   Populations in prison have tripled since the 1970s
  C.   Conditions of Confinement Lawsuits
    1.   Inmates frequently file conditions of confinement lawsuits
  D.   High Costs
    1.   Constructing new cells cost between $75,000 and $100,000
    2.   Costs of keeping a prisoner are between $25,000 and $30,000 per year

V.   **Probation**
  A.   Probation is the primary alternative to incarceration
  B.   Defendant remains in community with conditions and supervision

VI.   **Fines**
  A.   One of oldest forms of punishment
  B.   Many offenders are poor, but fines can be collected with proper programs

VII.   **Restitution**
  A.   Direct restitution, the offender makes monetary payments to victim
  B.   In symbolic restitution, the offender does community service work

VIII.   **Intermediate Sanctions**
  A.   Intermediate sanctions are those between probation and imprisonment
  B.   Less costly than prison but provide more control than probation
  C.   Community Service
    1.   Most visible when imposed on celebrities
  D.   Intensive Probation
    1.   Targets offenders likely to be imprisoned on next violation
  E.   Boot Camp
    1.   Shock incarceration for 30-90 days
    2.   Evaluations suggest boot camps are not effective and costly

IX.   **The Death Penalty**
  A.   Most controversial of all punishments
  B.   The U.S. is the only Western democracy still using it
  C.   Eighth Amendment Standards
    1.   In *Furman v. Ga.* (1972) the U.S. Supreme Court invalidated all state capital punishment laws
    2.   *Gregg v. Ga.* (1976) the Court validated guided discretion capital punishment laws
  B.   Contemporary Death Penalty Laws
    1.   38 states and federal government have death penalty
    2.   Capital punishment may only be inflicted for murder
    3.   Most executions occur in southern and western states

C.	Appeals and Evolving Standards
1.	Automatic revues of death sentences
2.	Eighth Amendment limits on capital punishment
a.	Persons fifteen or younger at time of murder cannot be executed
b.	Mentally retarded persons cannot be executed
D.	Death Row Inmates
1.	Currently about 3,300 prisoners on death row
b.	Most are male, minority, poor, and uneducated

X.	**Conclusion**

KEY TERMS

capital offense - Any crime punishable by death. (336)

capital punishment - Use of the death penalty as the punishment for the commission of a particular crime. (336)

conditions of confinement lawsuit - Lawsuit brought by a prisoner contesting prison conditions. (328)

cruel and unusual punishment - Governmental punishment that is prohibited by the Eighth Amendment. (327)

death penalty - Capital punishment, or executions by the state for purposes of social defense.(336)

determinate sentence - A term of imprisonment, imposed by a judge, that has a specific number of years. (324)

deterrence theory - The view that sure and swift punishment will discourage others from similar illegal acts. (321)

direct restitution - The defendant pays money directly to the victim of the crime. (333)

fine - A sum of money to be paid to the state by a convicted person as punishment for an offense. (333)

Furman v. Georgia - Supreme Court ruling that statutes leaving arbitrary and discriminatory discretion to juries in imposing death sentences are in violation of the Eighth Amendment. (337)

good time - A reduction of the time served in prison as a reward for not violating prison rules. (326)

Gregg v. Georgia - Supreme Court ruling that (1) the death penalty is not, in itself, cruel and unusual punishment, and (2) a two-part proceeding— one for the determination of innocence or guilt and the other for determination of the sentence—is constitutional and meets the objections noted in *Furman v. Georgia* (337)

imprisonment - Placing a person in a prison, jail, or similar correctional facility as punishment for committing a crime. (327)

incapacitation - Sentencing philosophy that stresses crime prevention through isolating wrongdoers from society. (321)

indeterminate sentence - A sentence that has both a minimum and a maximum term of imprisonment, the actual length to be determined by a parole board. (324)

intermediate sanctions - Variety of sanctions that lie somewhere between prison and probation. (334)

just deserts - Punishment for criminal wrongdoing should be proportionate to the severity of the offense. (321)

pardon - An act of executive clemency that has the effect of releasing an inmate from prison and/or removing certain legal disabilities from persons convicted of crimes. (326)

parole - Early release from prison on the condition of good behavior. (326)

parole board - An administrative body whose members are chosen by the governor to review the cases of prisoners eligible for release on parole. The board has the authority to release such persons and to return them to prison for violating the conditions of parole. (326)

probation - Punishment for a crime that allows the offender to remain in the community without incarceration but subject to certain conditions. (331)

rehabilitation - The notion that punishment is intended to restore offenders to a constructive role in society; based on the assumption that criminal behavior is a treatable disorder caused by social or psychological ailments. (322)

restitution - To restore or to make good on something— for example, to return or pay for a stolen item. (333)

retribution - A concept that implies the payment of a debt to society and thus the expiration of one's offense. (320)

selective incapacitation - Sentencing philosophy that stresses targeting dangerous offenders for lengthy prison sentences. (321)

symbolic restitution - The defendant performs community service. (334)

CHAPTER SUMMARY

During the last three decades, there has been an intense public debate over punishment philosophies. The previously dominant goal attempting to change offenders into law-abiding citizens (rehabilitation) has come under intense criticism. Many argue that retribution (an eye for an eye) or just deserts (criminals deserve to be punished) should be the goal. Incapacitating and deterring criminals are also popular theories.

For nearly 40 years, the indeterminate sentencing system dominated. It has now been rejected in many states. Determinate or fixed sentences have become more popular. The mix of sentencing authority has changed. Legislators have inserted themselves more directly in the sentencing process, reducing discretion of judges and parole boards.

One of the judge's sentencing options is imprisonment. Today we have over two million persons in prisons and jails. The U.S. imprisons persons at a higher rate than most industrialized countries and the costs are enormous. Prison overcrowding is a serious problem.

Probation is the primary alternative to prison. Offenders remain in the community with conditions and supervision. Today we have more than four million persons on probation. Fines and restitution to victims are also frequently used. Beginning in the 1960s, restitution became increasingly popular.

Intermediate sanctions are designed for those who do not warrant prison but need more control than ordinary probation. These sanctions include community service, intensive supervision probation (ISP), and boot camps. While the evaluations of intermediate sanctions are mixed, there is little evidence to suggest they are very effective. ISP might even lead to increased prison populations since offenders often fail to meet their probation conditions and are remanded to prison.

All state death penalty laws were struck down by the U.S. Supreme Court in 1972 in *Furman v. Ga*. Later, guided discretion statutes were upheld but mandatory death penalty statutes were struck down. Today, thirty-eight states and the federal government have the death penalty. However, the Eighth Amendment prohibits execution of the mentally retarded and those under fifteen years of age when the crime was committed. It also appears that murder may be the only crime for which this penalty can be exacted.

Today there are around 3,300 prisoners on death row. Most are minority males with little education and prior felony convictions. Due to the lengthy appeals process, the average person executed had been on death row a little over seven years. Roughly a third of persons on death row will escape execution through legal means or will die in prison.

PRACTICE TEST BANK

Multiple Choice

1. A sentence of ten to fifteen years imprisonment is a/n _____ sentence.
    a. fixed
    b. indeterminate
    c. mandatory minimum
    d. determinate

2. Which type of crime would be most amenable to restorative justice approaches?
    a. rape and murder of a child
    b. espionage
    c. family violence
    d. sedition

3. Restitution is most consistent with the punishment theory of _____.
    a. retribution
    b. rehabilitation
    c. deterrence
    d. incapacitation

4. _____ incapacitation focuses on offenders with a high potential for serious recidivism.
    a. Focused
    b. Special
    c. Preferential
    d. Selective

5. Deterrence theory was advocated by _____, a nineteenth century British criminologist.
    a. Jeremy Bentham
    b. Thomas Aquinas
    b. John Stuart Mill
    c. Jacques Rousseau

6. Beginning in the mid 1970s, the trend in sentencing has been toward _____.
    a. greater emphasis rehabilitation
    b. increasing the use of indeterminate sentences
    c. decreasing judicial and parole board discretion
    d. discounting deterrence and incapacitation

7. A determinate or ____ sentence is a sentence of a specific number of years imprisonment.
    a. fixed
    b. indefinite
    c. definite
    d. indeterminate

8. Wide sentencing discretion and making the punishment fit the criminal is least consistent with _____.
    a. general deterrence
    b. rehabilitation
    c. retribution
    d. restorative justice

9. The legislative branch's influence on punishment is exercised through _____.
    a. restorative justice programs
    b. parole boards and pardons
    c. common law writs
    d. mandatory minimum and determinate sentencing schemes

10. A tooth-for-a-tooth is an example of punishment based on _____.
    a. rehabilitation
    b. retribution
    c. incapacitation
    d. deterrence

11. The most ancient justification for punishment is _____.
    a. rehabilitation
    b. deterrence
    c. retribution
    d. incapacitation

12. Cruel and unusual punishments are prohibited by the _____ Amendment.
    a. Sixth
    b. Eighth
    c. Ninth
    d. Tenth

13. Symbolic_____ commonly involves some form of community service.
    a. fines
    b. retribution
    c. rehabilitation
    d. restitution

14. Today, _____ states and the federal government have capital punishment laws.
    a. only a few
    b. about a dozen
    c. fewer than half the
    d. more than half the

15. The majority of individuals on death row are _____.
    a. white
    b. nonwhite
    c. females
    d. high school graduates

16. How many offenders were on death row by the end of 2002?
    a. 6754
    b. 4719
    c. 2713
    d. 671

17. Research on the effect of deterrence shows _____.
    a. no deterrent effects
    b. consistently strong effects
    c. that deterrence works only with young people
    d. inconsistent results

18. Beginning around 1975, trends in prison populations showed _____.
    a. marked decreases
    b. marked increases
    c. slight decreases
    d. slight increases

19. Today, on average per year, it costs between ____ thousand dollars to keep a person in prison.
    a. 20-30
    b. 30-40
    c. 40-50
    d. 50-60

20. Before the introduction of intermediate sanctions, judges usually had only a choice between probation and _____.
    a. parole
    b. banishment
    c. house arrest and electronic monitoring
    d. incarceration

True-False

1. A disproportionate number of people on death row are white.
   a. true
   b false

2. Most prisoners on death row have no prior felony convictions.
   a. true
   b. false

3.   The theory of just deserts is generally consistent with retribution.
        a.   true
        b.   false

4.   Rehabilitation was championed by English criminologist Jeremy Bentham.
        a.   true
        b.   false

5.   Retribution focuses on the criminal rather than the crime committed.
        a.   true
        b.   false

6.   The legislative branch of government becomes involved in punishment by way of pardons and parole.
        a.   true
        b.   false

7.   The Eighth Amendment prohibits cruel and unusual punishment.
        a.   true
        b.   false

8.   In *Atkins v. Va.*, the U.S. Supreme Court held that offenders under sixteen cannot be executed.
        a.   true
        b.   false

9.   American prison populations have been declining since 1985.
        a.   true
        b.   false

10.   Intermediate sanctions are sanctions between ordinary probation and prison.
        a.   true
        b.   false

11.   Most offenders on death row have completed high school.
        a.   true
        b.   false

12.   Banishment and transportation are historical examples of retribution.
        a.   true
        b.   false

13.   Indefinite sentences are often referred to as determinate sentences.
        a.   true
        b.   false

14. In recent years, good time laws and parole have been instituted or expanded in many jurisdictions.
   a. true
   b. false

15 The East has more people in prison under sentence of death than any of the three other regions in the U.S.
   a. true
   b. false

Fill in the Blank

1. Fixed sentences are also referred to as _____ sentences.

2. The _____ Amendment prohibits cruel and unusual punishments.

3. To win a conditions of confinement lawsuit, the prisoners must show that prison officials acted with _____ indifference.

4. In _____ v. Va., the U.S. Supreme Court held that mentally retarded offenders with an IQ of seventy or lower cannot be executed.

5. A sentence is one with a minimum and maximum term is a/n _____ sentence.

6. _____ is a form of conditional release from prison with supervision.

7. _____ have authority to issue pardons to convicted state offenders.

8. _____ deserts theory is similar to retribution.

9. _____ sanctions are punishments between ordinary probation and prison.

10. Prisoners may advance their date of release from prison by earning good _____.

11. _____ involves an offender making compensatory monetary payments to the victim.

12. _____ incapacitation involves attempting to predict which offenders have the highest probability of recidivism.

13. _____ is the theory that fear of punishment will prevent crime.

14. The Old Testament theory of punishment is _____.

15. Retribution and just deserts require that the punishment be _____ to the harm.

<u>Essay</u>

1.   Define and discuss intermediate sanctions. What are the rationales for such sanctions? Be sure to provide examples.

2.   What are the current trends in and costs of imprisoning offenders? Do you think we over utilize prison sentences. Explain your position. Do you think the costs are worth it? Explain your position.

3.   Define, discuss, compare and contrast probation, parole and pardon. Be sure to provide examples.

4.   Discuss the general demographic characteristics of persons on death row. What does this data suggest about the penalty? What does this data suggest about who commits capital crimes?

5.   Compare and contrast deterrence, incapacitation, rehabilitation and retribution. Be sure to provide examples of each. Which of these four do you think should be the dominant sentencing consideration? Explain your position.

CHAPTER 15 ANSWER KEYS

Multiple Choice

1—d	2—c	3—a	4—d	5—a
6—c	7—a	8—b	9—d	10—b
11—c	12—b	13—d	14—d	15—a
16—a	17—d	18—b	19—a	20—d

True-False

1—F	2—F	3—T	4—F	5—F
6—F	7—T	8—F	9—F	10—T
11—F	12—F	13—F	14—F	15—F

Fill in the blank

1—determinate	2—Eighth	3—deliberate	4—Atkins
5—indeterminate	6—parole	7—Governors	8—Just
9—intermediate	10—time	11—restitution	12—selective
13—deterrence	14—retribution	15—proportional	

Chapter 16
SENTENCING DECISIONS

LEARNING OBJECTIVES

After reading this chapter, student should understand the

- role of the courtroom work group and sentencing decisions.
- considerations used in making sentencing decisions.
- various discriminating factors that affect sentencing decisions.
- nature of social factors and their impact on discrimination within the sentencing process.
- extent of sentencing disparities.
- changing nature of sentencing structures.
- impact of state and federal sentencing guidelines.
- controversy surrounding increasing the severity of penalties.

CHAPTER OUTLINE

I. **Courtroom Work Groups and Sentencing Decisions**
    A.   Probation Officers
        1.   Creates presentence investigation and report for judge
        2.   Plays a significant role in the sentencing process
    B.   Prosecutors
        1.   May engage in plea bargaining to shape or determine the sentence
    C.   Defense Attorneys
        1.   Entire strategy depends heavily on potential sentence
        2.   Less influential than prosecutor
    D.   Judges
        1.   Have final authority
        2.   Influenced by work group norms

II. **Normal Penalties and Sentencing Decisions**
    A.   Most cases involve familiar patterns and concepts of normal or average sentences emerge
    B.   Seriousness of the Offense
        1.   Most important factor in sentencing
    C.   Prior Record
        1.   Prior record increases sentences
    D.   Aggravating or Mitigating Circumstances
        1.   Age, mental capacity, role in the crime (principal or secondary)
    E.   Law in Controversy: Uncertainty and Public Opinion
        1.   Sentencing is more art than science
        2.   Public largely believes sentencing is too lenient

III. **Discrimination and Sentencing**
    A.   Refers to illegitimate influences on the sentencing process
    B.   Imbalance versus Discrimination

1. Some research shows discrimination based on race, ethnicity etc; other research does not support race as a factor

C. Conflicting Findings

IV. Discrimination and Economic Status

A. Discrimination against the poor and unemployed may stem from legitimate indicators of social stability *(e.g.,* steady employment)

B. *Social dynamite*

V. Discrimination and Gender

A. Why Are Women Increasingly Being Sentenced to Prison?
1. War on drugs

B Are Women Sentenced More Leniently Than Men?
1. Women more likely to receive probation
   a. Chivalry
   b. Evil woman
   c. Equal treatment

VI. Discrimination and Race

A. Racial discrimination
1. Research results are inconsistent

VII. Discrimination and Capital Punishment

A. 72 percent of those executed in the South were black between 1930 and 1966

B. Offender-Victim Dyad
1. Blacks killing or raping whites most likely to receive the death penalty

C. Evidence of Discrimination Since *Gregg*
1. Prosecutors more likely to request death penalties for Blacks

D. Evidence of No Discrimination Since *Gregg*
1. Nonprimary homicides most likely to receive the death penalty (strangers)

E. *McCleskey v. Kemp* Bars Social Science Evidence
1. (1987) Supreme Court rejected statistical evidence of racial bias in death penalty

VIII. Disparities and Sentencing

A. Disparity refers to inconsistencies in sentencing

B. The Geography of Justice
1. South imposes harsher sentences than other regions

C. Judges' Backgrounds and Attitudes
1. Sentences of most judges fall somewhere in between the extremes of leniency and harsh sentencers

IX. Changing Sentencing Structures

A. Both liberals and conservatives criticized prior practices that appeared to result in discrimination and disparity and excessive leniency

    B.   Law in Controversy: Reducing Judicial Discretion

          1.   Many jurisdictions eliminated indeterminate sentencing, which gave power of release to parole boards

    C.   Law on the Books: Determinate Sentencing Returns

          1.   In response to the rehabilitation model, many jurisdictions have moved to determinate (fixed) sentencing with abolition or reduction of parole

    D.   Law in Action: Diverse Impacts

          1.   Reforms (and sentencing guidelines) have generally resulted in longer sentences and swelling prison populations

X.   **Sentencing Guidelines**

    A.   State Sentencing Guidelines

          1.   Voluntary/mandatory guidelines

               a.   Presumptive or mandatory guidelines must be followed by judges

               b.   Voluntary guidelines have had little impact, mandatory guidelines have changed judicial behavior and resulted in more severe sentences

          2.   In 2004, the Court struck down sentencing guidelines in Washington state

    B.   Federal Sentencing Guidelines

          1.   U.S. v. Booker (2005) the Court ruled sentencing guidelines unconstitutional and too harsh

XI.   **Increasing the Severity of the Penalty**

    A.   Law on the Books: Mandatory Minimum Sentences

          1.   Discretion by criminal justice officials allows side-stepping of these laws

          2.   Judges dislike curtailment of their discretion

          3.   Three strikes laws generally provide life sentences for persons with prior felony convictions

    B.   Law in Action: Nullification by Discretion

          1.   Decrease in filing of charges by prosecutors

    C.   Law in Controversy: Negative Side Effects

          1.   Defendants may demand trials now because of harsher punishments, putting a burden on the system

          2.   Rigid and inflexible sentences may cause injustices in particular cases

          3.   Prison overcrowding, construction and related costs are serious concerns

XII.   **Conclusion**

          1.   Public wants harsh punishment but is resistant to raising taxes to build new prisons and fund new programs

---

KEY TERMS

discrimination - Illegitimate influences in the sentencing process based on the characteristics of the defendants. (354)

disparity - Unequal sentences resulting from the sentencing process itself. (360)

mandatory minimum sentencing - Minimum required penalty specified for a certain crime. (368)

normal penalties - Norms for proper sentencing based on the crime committed and the defendant's prior record. (351)

pre-sentence investigation - Investigation by a probation department into circumstances surrounding a crime in order to help judges make appropriate sentencing decisions. (348)

sentencing guidelines - Recommended sentences based on the severity of the crime and the defendant's prior record in an attempt to ensure fair and consistent sentencing. (364)

CHAPTER SUMMARY

Whether the "three strikes" and other get-tough laws passed in the aftermath of the Polly Klaas kidnapping and murder will have a lasting or beneficial impact is questionable. The public reaction and expectation regarding punishment is skewed by the sensational cases that do not reflect most defendants. "Get tough" policies are popular among politicians. However, judges must deal with real-life defendants, limited budgets, overworked probation officers and overcrowded prisons. Judges must wrestle with the sentence to impose on almost 900,000 felons convicted every year.

In deciding whether to send an offender to prison or grant probation, the judge and members of the courtroom work group attempt to balance a number of factors. Normal penalties are the most important consideration in sentencing. Based on the seriousness of the offense and the defendant's prior record, courthouses have developed going rates, which are used as parameters in fine-tuning a sentence for a given offender. The norms of the group are the primary determinant of the sentence in the overwhelming majority of cases.

The probation officer becomes an important member of the courtroom workgroup when sentencing is involved. This official does a presentence investigation and provides the judge with a report. The report may include a recommendation as to sentence. Probation officers also supervise defendants placed on probation.

Sentencing practices are highly controversial. To some, sentencing decisions do not constitute fair and impartial justice. Sentencing disparity is a concern. Laws and judges are more harsh is some jurisdictions than others. Judicial attitudes also influence sentencing. Some criticize sentences by alleging that they are discriminatory. Discriminatory sentencing is sentencing which is based on illegal considerations such as race, ethnicity, gender etc. Numerous studies have probed the extent to which economic status, age, gender, and race improperly influence the sentence. The results of such studies are mixed. Others see sentences as being too lenient. These two concerns have prompted numerous changes since the mid 1970s.

Determinate sentencing laws, mandatory minimum sentencing provisions, and sentencing guidelines are now common at both the state and federal levels. However, the Court has taken a stance that some guidelines are unconstitutional in that they are too harsh or only juries rather than judges can extend sentences beyond the guideline recommendations. Three-strikes laws have become popular and have been upheld by the U.S. Supreme Court. Parole has been abolished or limited, and sentencing guidelines and truth in sentencing laws have resulted in longer sentences.

Prison populations are increasing. The United States sends more people to prison than any other Western nation, and the rate of incarceration is increasing steadily. The result is severe prison overcrowding, compounded by federal court orders requiring major improvements in prison conditions. The financial costs of such mass imprisonment are staggering. Although taxpayers want longer and harsher sentences, they are unwilling to spend the large sums of money needed to build adequate facilities and provide programs for inmates.

PRACTICE TEST BANK

Multiple Choice

1. Which of the following is a consequence of sentencing guidelines and mandatory minimum sentencing laws?
    a. fewer plea bargains
    b. fewer trials.
    c. fewer women in prison
    d. lower taxes

2. The term "normal crime" is used to describe _____ penalties appropriate for various categories of offenders and offenses.
    a. sentencing guideline
    b. public opinion about
    c. courtroom work group norms about
    d. Supreme Court Justices' attitudes regarding

3. The _____ model of sentencing is based on the principle of just deserts.
    a. due process
    b. justice
    c. neo-incorporation
    d. rehabilitative

4. In most _____ sentencing schemes, the offender is released from prison when the parole board grants parole.
    a. determinate
    b. mandatory minimum
    c. sentencing guidelines
    d. indeterminate

5. _____ in sentencing is caused by different laws in different jurisdictions and/or judicial attitudes toward sentencing.
    a. Disparity
    b. Discrimination
    c. Discrepancies
    d. Dissolution

6. In _____(1987), the U.S. Supreme Court refused to overturn the death sentence because the social science evidence did not show discrimination in this particular case.
    a. *Gregg v. Ga.*
    b. *Doe v. Connecticut*
    c. *McCleskey v. Kemp*
    d. *Mistretta v. U.S.*

7. For the courtroom workgroup, the most important factor in sentencing is the _____.
    a. prior record of the offender
    b. skill of the defense attorney
    c. victim's need for restitution
    d. seriousness of the offense

8. Capital punishment research on the offender-victim racial dyad established that cases involving _____ were least likely to result in the death penalty as compared to other dyads.
    a. black offenders and white victims
    b. white offenders and white victims
    c. black offenders and black victims
    d. white offenders and black victims

9   Truth-in-sentencing laws are sometimes also referred to as _____ sentencing laws.
    a. indeterminate
    b. determinate
    c. mandatory minimum
    d. Megan's

10. In a 1994 dissenting opinion, Supreme Court Justice Harry Blackmun concluded that Supreme Court attempts to produce fairness in _____ had failed.
    a. sentencing guidelines
    b. imposition of the death penalty
    c. capital punishment for rape
    d. indeterminate sentencing

11. A majority of Americans believe that the length of prison sentences is _____.
    a. too harsh
    b. too lenient
    c. consistent with retribution, deterrence and incapacitation
    d. is satisfactory

12. In general, in the U.S. the rates of imprisonment are highest in the _____.
    a. Pacific northwest
    b. Southern states
    c. New England
    d. upper Midwest

13. In *Ewing v. California*, the U.S. Supreme Court held that California's three strikes law did not violate the _____ Amendment.
    a. Eighth
    b. Ninth
    c. Tenth
    d. Eleventh

14. A _____ is a sentence for a specific term of years (*e.g.*, 10 years) that is within the legislatively prescribed range.
    a. indeterminate
    b. mandatory minimum
    c. determinate
    d. indefinite

15. Based on research results on gender discrimination in sentencing, most experts now _____.
    a. accept the evil woman theory and reject the chivalry/paternalism theory
    b. accept both the evil woman and chivalry/paternalism theory
    c. reject both the evil woman and chivalry/paternalism theory
    d. reject the evil woman theory but accept the chivalry/paternalism theory

16. In *Mistretta v. U.S.* (1989), the U.S. Supreme Court held that the federal sentencing guidelines did not violate the doctrine of _____.
    a. separation of powers
    b. individualized sentencing
    c. *res ipsa loquitur*
    d. federalism

17. The two primary factors in most sentencing guidelines are _____.
    a. seriousness of offense and criminal history
    b. incapacitation and rehabilitation
    c special and general deterrence
    d available prison space and parole caseloads

18. The rape and murder of seven year-old Polly Klaas created public and political support for _____.
    a. mandatory minimum sentencing
    b. sentencing guidelines
    c. presumptive sentencing
    d. sex-offender registration laws

19. Federal court sentencing guidelines _____.
    a. have reduced federal prison populations
    b. are popular with criminal defendants
    c. are criticized for allowing too much discretion and too much leniency
    d. are criticized as unfair, rigid, harsh and complex

20 Many have suggested that Lady Justice appears to cost more than:
    a. citizens can afford
    b. the public is willing to spend
    c. most citizens can earn
    d. the cost of policing

True-False

1.   Most Americans believe that prison sentences are too harsh.
      a.   true
      b.   false

2.   In recent years, male prison populations have been growing faster than female prison populations.
      a.   true
      b.   false

3.   Overall, the Southern states impose the harshest punishments for crime.
      a.   true
      b.   false

4.   Three-strikes laws were validated by the U.S. Supreme Court in 2002 in *Ewing v. California*.
      a.   true
      b.   false

5.   The U.S. Supreme Court held in *Mistretta v. U.S.* that the federal sentencing guidelines did not violate separation of powers.
      a.   true
      b.   false

6.   Sentencing guidelines are associated with decreasing severity of sentences.
      a.   true
      b.   false

7.   In the U.S., get-tough punishment laws and the war on drugs have increased prison populations.
      a.   true
      b.   false

8.   Judges sentence over 1,800,000 convicted felons each year.
      a.   true
      b.   false

9.   Data shows that the overwhelming majority of persons sentenced in state courts for felony property offenses get probation.
      a.   true
      b.   false

10.   The research results overwhelmingly prove nationwide discrimination in sentencing.
      a.   true
      b.   false

11.   Contemporary research shows strong support for the chivalry theory of female sentencing.
       a.   true
       b.   false

12.   The most important factor in setting normal penalties is the seriousness of the offense.
       a.   true
       b.   false

13.   In spite of aggregate statistical evidence of racial discrimination, the U.S. Supreme Court refused to strike down Georgia's capital punishment statute in *McCleskey v. Kemp*.
       a.   true
       b.   false

14.   Sentencing patterns based on extralegal/unlawful factors is termed sentencing discrimination.
       a.   true
       b.   false

15.   The trend since the 1970s has been to increase judicial discretion in sentencing.
       a.   true
       b.   false

Fill in the Blank

1.   Research suggests that the death penalty is least likely to be inflicted in cases involving a white offender and a _____ victim.

2.   The chivalry or_____ theory suggests that women will generally get more lenient treatment in the criminal justice system than men.

3.   A sentencing system in which the amount of time served is ultimately decided by a parole board is called an _____ sentencing system.

4.   The two main types of sentencing guidelines are presumptive and _____.

5.   A sentence of five years imprisonment is a _____ sentence.

6.   Judges in Minnesota, the federal government and many states use sentencing _____ to impose sentences.

7.   In *Ewing v. Calif.* (2002), the U.S. Supreme Court held that California's _____law did not violate the Eighth Amendment.

8.   By focusing on the "_____ offense," judges can counteract charge bargaining.

9.   Age, low I.Q., and marginal participation in the crime are _____ factors at sentencing.

10. Federal penalties for possession of crack are harsher than the penalties for equivalent amounts of _____

11. Presentence investigation reports are written by _____ officers.

12. Guided discretion death penalty statutes were upheld by the U.S. Supreme Court in _____ v. *Georgia* (1976).

13. The U.S. Supreme Court struck down state death penalty laws in 1972 in _____ v. *Georgia*.

14. In New Jersey in 1994, _____ law required registration of sex offenders.

15. Objectionable and illegal variables that result in sentencing discrimination are called _____ variables.

Essay

1. Describe how indeterminate sentencing systems work. Be sure to provide examples.

2. Discuss the liberal and conservative critique of indeterminate sentencing laws. Be sure to provide examples. Which, if any, of these critiques do you find reasonable? Be sure to explain your position.

3. What is the "geography of justice? Be sure to provide examples.

4. Compare and contrast determinate and indeterminate sentences. Be sure to provide examples.

5. Compare and contrast sentencing discrimination and sentencing disparity. Be sure to provide examples.

CHAPTER 16 ANSWER KEYS

<u>Multiple Choice</u>

1—a	2—c	3—b	4—d	5—a
6—c	7—d	8—d	9—c	10—b
11—b	12—b	13—a	14—d	15—c
16—a	17—a	18—d	19—d	20—b

<u>True-False</u>

1—F	2—F	3—T	4—T	5—T
6—F	7—T	8—F	9—F	10—F
11—F	12—T	13—T	14—T	15—F

<u>Fill in the blank</u>

1—black	2—paternalistic	3—indeterminate	4—voluntary
5—determinate	6—guidelines	7—three-strikes	8—real
9—mitigating	10—cocaine	11—probation	12—Gregg
13—Furman	14—Megan's	15—extralegal	

Chapter 17
APPELLATE COURTS

After reading this chapter, students should understand the
- nature and extent of the appellate process.
- various processes used for appealing a criminal case.
- rulings commonly rendered by appellate courts.
- post conviction reviews differ from appeals.
- role and function of state supreme courts in the appeals process.
- historical evolution of the modern U.S. Supreme Court.
- the impact of the Court's justice policies on our criminal justice system.

CHAPTER OUTLINE

I. **Nature of the Appellate Process**
    A.   Notion of several heads being better than one
    B.   The Purposes of Appeal
        1.   Correct errors made by lower courts
        2.   Formulate legal policy
    C.   Scope of Appellate Review
        1.   Losing parties have a minimum right of one appeal
        2.   General rule is that interlocutory (nonfinal) orders cannot be appealed
        3.   Two types of appellate jurisdiction
            a.   Mandatory—court must hear appeal
            b.   Discretionary—court may choose which appeals to hear

II. **Appellate Court Procedures**
    A.   Notice of Appeal (appellant)
    B.   Appellate Record
    C.   Briefing the Case (appellee)
    D.   Oral Argument
        1.   Appellant and appellee argue cases in person before judges
    E.   Written Opinion
        1.   Majority opinion announces decision
        2.   Dissenting opinions express disagreement with majority
    F.   Disposition
        1.   Affirmed—appellate court agrees with lower court
        2.   Reversed—appellate court overturns decision of lower court
        3.   Remanded—case sent back to lower court for further action
        4.   Reversible error—error by lower court requires new trial
        5.   Harmless error—error not serious enough to change result

III. **Criminal Appeals**
    A.   Law on the Books: Expanded Opportunity to Appeal Criminal Convictions

1.   Warren Court decisions provided additional grounds for criminal appeals and free services to indigent convicts

B.   Law in Action: Defendants Rarely Win on Appeal

1.   Defendants win on appeal only about one out of eight times

IV. Post-Conviction Review

A.   *Collateral attacks* by prison inmates

B.   How Post-Conviction Remedies Differ from Appeals

1.   Only filed by those in prison

2.   Only constitutional defects

3.   Broader than appeals

C.   Expansion under the Warren Court

1.   Warren Court expanded use of *habeas corpus*

D.   Contraction under the Burger and Rehnquist Courts

1.   Conservative Rehnquist and Burger Courts have limited *habeas corpus*

E.   Congress Greatly Restricts Federal Habeas

1.   Congress has also limited ability of inmates to use *habeas corpus*

V. State Supreme Courts

A.   Law on the Books: State Supreme Courts and Discretionary Dockets

1.   40 states have intermediate appellate courts with appellate jurisdiction

2.   Appellate courts of last resort have much discretionary jurisdiction

B.   Law in Action: State Supreme Courts as Policymakers

1.   As U.S. Supreme Court turned conservative, liberals and progressives turned to state supreme courts

2.   New judicial federalism—liberal and conservative state supreme courts use state constitutions to make policy

C.   Law in Controversy: State Supreme Courts and Death Penalty Cases

1.   Liberal and progressive judges and courts tend to overturn death sentences

2.   Conservative judges and courts tend to uphold death sentences

VI. The U.S. Supreme Court and Criminal Justice Policy

A.   Only about 26 criminal cases are reviewed by the Court with full opinion

B.   The Warren Court (1953-1969)

1.   Expanded civil liberties and rights of individuals and criminal defendants

C.   The Burger Court (1969-1986)

1.   More conservative than Warren Court and reinstated the death penalty

D.   The Rehnquist Court (1986-2005)

1.   Conservative court on many issues

      a.   Conservatives—Rehnquist, Scalia, Thomas, and occasionally Kennedy

      b.   Liberals—Stevens, Ginsburg, Breyer and Souter

      c.   Swing votes—O'Connor and sometimes Kennedy

2.   In *Bush v. Gore* (2000) conservatives hand election to Bush with dissention of liberal members

E. The Roberts Court (2005-   )
    1. Predicted to be a very conservative court
F. The Supreme Court in Broad Perspective
    1. Overall, Supreme Court decisions swing like a pendulum from liberal to moderate to conservative and then back again

VII. Conclusion

KEY TERMS

affirm - In an appellate court, to reach a decision that agrees with the result reached in the case by the lower court. (382)

appellant - The party, usually the losing one, that seeks to overturn the decision of a lower court by appealing to a higher court. (380)

appellate court record - Papers, documents, and exhibits, as well as the transcript of the trial, that are submitted to the appellate court for review. (381)

appellee **(respondent)** - A party, usually the winning party, against whom a case is appealed. (382)

brief - A written statement submitted by the attorney arguing a case in court. It states the facts of the case, presents legal arguments in support of the moving party, and cites applicable law. (382)

Burger Court - The Supreme Court under the leadership of Chief Justice Warren Burger (1969–1986). (393)

discretionary appellate jurisdiction - Jurisdiction that a court may accept or reject in particular cases. The Supreme Court has discretionary jurisdiction over most cases that come to it. (380)

dissenting opinion - An opinion written by a judge of an appellate court in which the judge states the reasons for disagreeing with the majority decision. (382)

double jeopardy - Fifth Amendment prohibition against a second prosecution after a first trial for the same offense. (379)

en banc - French term referring to the session of an appellate court in which all the judges of the court participate, as opposed to a session presided over by three judges. (378)

error - A mistake made by a judge in the procedures used at trial, or in making legal rulings during the trial, that allows one side in a lawsuit to ask a higher court to review the case. (382)

error correction - Appellate courts seek to correct legal errors made in lower courts. (378)

habeas corpus - Latin phrase meaning "you have the body"; a writ inquiring of an official who has custody of a person whether that person is being lawfully imprisoned or detained. (387)

harmless error - An error made at trial that is insufficient grounds for reversing a judgment. (382)

interlocutory - Provisional; temporary; while a lawsuit is still going on. (379)

mandatory appellate jurisdiction - Jurisdiction that a court must accept. Cases falling under a court's mandatory jurisdiction must be decided officially on their merits, though a court may avoid giving them full consideration. (379)

new judicial federalism - Movement in state supreme courts to reinvigorate states' constitutions as sources of individual rights over and above the rights granted by the U.S. Constitution. (390)

notice of appeal - Written document filed with the clerk of court stating that the defendant in the criminal case plans to appeal. (380)

opinion - The reasons given for the decision reached by an appellate court. (382)

oral argument - The part of the appellate court decision-making process in which lawyers for both parties plead their case in person before the court. (382)

policy formulation - Function of appellate courts to make new law and adjust existing law to changing circumstances. (378)

Rehnquist Court - The Supreme Court under the leadership of Chief Justice William Rehnquist (1986–2005). (394)

Roberts Court - The Supreme Court under the leadership of Chief Justice John Roberts (2005–). (395)

remand - In an appellate court, to send a case back to the court from which it came for further action. (382)

reverse - In an appellate court, to reach a decision that disagrees with the result reached in the case by the lower court. (382)

reversed and remanded - Decision of an appellate court that the guilty verdict of the lower court be set aside and the case be retried. (382)

reversible error - An error made at trial serious enough to warrant a new trial. (382)

right to one appeal - U.S. law generally grants the loser in trial court the right to a single appeal, which the upper court must hear. (378)

Warren Court - The Supreme Court under the leadership of Chief Justice Earl Warren (1953–1969). (393)

CHAPTER SUMMARY

In the American judicial process, every loser in a civil trial court gets the right to at least one appeal to a higher court, while in a criminal trial, only the defendant has that right. Appellate courts operate on the belief that several judges are better than one. On appeal, the decisions of a single judge are subjected to review by a panel of judges who are removed from heat generated by the controversy and are thus in a position to take a more objective approach. Most states have intermediate appellate courts and then a court of last resort, usually a Supreme Court. In intermediate appellate courts, decisions are usually made by rotating three-judge panels. However, in important cases all judges may participate *(en banc* hearing). The most obvious function of appellate courts is to correct errors made by the courts below. The other primary function is making policy.

Most of the jurisdiction of intermediate appellate courts is mandatory. This means that they must decide all cases properly appealed to them. Most of the jurisdiction of courts of last resort (supreme courts) is discretionary—they can pick and choose which appeals to hear.

The party who lost at the lower or current level has the option to appeal. The first step is filing a notice of appeal. This party is called the appellant or petitioner. The party who won and is opposing the appeal is the appellee or respondent. The parties will file written arguments (briefs) with the appellate court and may have the opportunity to make an oral presentation (oral argument).

In most cases, the appellate court will write an opinion explaining and justifying its decision. The majority opinion establishes the law and precedent. Judges who disagree may file dissenting opinions. An error in the court below that requires that the court below be reversed is called a reversible error. An error that does not require overturning the lower court decision is called a harmless error. If the appellate court agrees with the lower court, the appellate court will affirm. The appellate court may also remand the case back to a lower court for further action.

Although most appeals are civil, criminal appeals have been growing rapidly since the 1960s. Appellate caseloads have been growing faster than trial caseloads, and many appellate courts are providing for expedited procedures.

Although many convicts appeal, only about one in eight wins on appeal. After exhausting appeals, convicts can use post-convictions remedies or *habeas corpus* to challenge the validity of their conviction. The rise in appeals and *habeas corpus* actions began with the Warren Court (1954-1963), which greatly expanded the rights of defendants and the use of *habeas corpus*. Later courts and Congress have limited the rights of appeal and *habeas corpus*.

State Supreme Courts have also been active policy-makers in their states. As the U.S. Supreme Court turned conservative, liberals and progressives turned to state courts and state constitutions for remedies. The term new judicial federalism was used to describe this phenomenon of using state constitutions to expand rights beyond those granted by the U.S. Constitution. However, research shows that both liberal and conservative judges have made use of this new activism.

Liberal state courts and judges have generally been hostile to the death penalty, while conservatives have shown the opposite reaction.

Because it has the final say on the meaning of the Constitution, which is the supreme law of the land, the U.S. Supreme Court has been extremely important in shaping criminal justice policy. The Warren Court often considered a liberal court, expanded civil rights and the rights of defendants. The more moderate Burger Court did not create the expected conservative counter-revolution many expected. However, the Rehnquist Court (1986-2005) has been generally conservative in most of their decisions. The current Roberts Court (2005-   ) is composed of conservatives: Roberts, Thomas, Scalia, and Alito with Kennedy sometimes joining them. There is a liberal bloc of Souter, Breyer, Ginsburg and Stevens.

PRACTICE TEST BANK

Multiple Choice

1.   During the Rehnquist Court, the deciding vote was frequently held by former Justice _____.
        a.   O'Connor.
        b.   Scalia.
        c.   Rehnquist.
        d.   Stevens.

2.   The current Chief Justice of the U.S. Supreme Court is _____.
        a.   Ruth Ginsburg
        b.   David Souter
        c.   Thurgood Marshall
        d.   John Roberts

3.   Which of the following is a fundamental purpose of the appellate courts?
        a.   training lower court judges
        b.   enforcing judgments
        c.   controlling jurisdiction
        d.   error correction

4.   At an _____ hearing, the appeal is heard by all the judges on the appellate court.
        a.   unanimous panel
        b.   *en banc*
        c.   majority
        d.   *dictu*

5.   One basic principle of American legal procedure is that the losing party is entitled to _____.
        a.   a writ of *certiorari*
        b.   *habeas corpus*
        c.   one appeal
        d.   *coram nobis*

6.   Most intermediate courts decisions are rendered by three judge _____.
        a.   panels
        b.   triumvirates
        c   convocations
        d.   invocations

7.   A court, which is required to hear an appeal is said to have ____ appellate jurisdiction.
        a.   compulsory
        b.   involuntary
        c.   mandatory
        d.   prescriptive

8. The party who won in the lower court and opposes the appeal is called the respondent or _____.
    a. petitioners
    b. appellee
    c. appellant
    d. party *ad litem*

9. If an appellate court reverses the lower court, this means that the appellate court _____.
    a. is issuing an opinion in the case
    b. aggress with the lower court decision
    c. disagrees with the lower court decision
    d. has decided not to hear the appeal

10. A legal error by the court below that requires that the lower court decision be overturned is called a _____ error.
    a. harmless
    b. moot
    c. reversible
    d. frivolous

11. In criminal case appeals, defendants win only about _____ time(s) in eight.
    a. 1
    b. 2
    c. 3
    d. 4

12. The first step in the appeal process is filing a notice of _____.
    a. error
    b. appeal
    c. disagreement
    d. challenge

13. The documents filed with the appellate court which contain legal arguments are called _____.
    a. arguments of error
    b. requests for judgment
    c. briefs
    d. notices

14. The Burger and Rehnquist Courts and U.S. Congress generally have _____.
    a. restricted the ability to appeal diversity jurisdiction cases
    b. cut back on the criminal jurisdiction of federal courts
    c. restricted *habeas corpus*
    d. increased the scope of post-conviction review

15. The Warren Court was followed by the more conservative _____ Court.
    a. Rehnquist
    b. Vinson
    c. Burger
    d. Kerry

16. The most controversial decision of the _____ Court was *Roe v. Wade*.
    a. Rehnquist
    b. Vinson
    c. Burger
    d. Warren

17. The new judicial _____ involves state courts using state constitutions to make public policy or strengthen rights.
    a. activism
    b. federalism
    c. usurpation
    d. restraints

18. A party may appeal only issues or questions of _____.
    a. law
    b. jurisdiction
    c. fact
    d. constitutional dimension

19. A court that has choices as to which appeals it will hear is said to have _____ appellate jurisdiction.
    a. optional
    b. prescient
    c. discretionary
    d. optional

20. State appellate courts decide _____ thousand appeals per year.
    a. 276
    b. 375
    c. 475
    d. 575

True-False

1. In 2004, there were three female Justices on the U.S. Supreme Court.
    a. true
    b. false

2. The Rehnquist Court was considered more liberal than the Warren Court.
    a. true
    b. false

3. State courts hear more appeals than federal courts.
    a. true
    b. false

4. Warren Court decisions in the 1960s resulted in more criminal appeals.
    a. true
    b. false

5. The most common type of post-conviction relief is *corpus delicti*.
    a. true
    b. false

6. The Burger Court failed to institute a constitutional counterrevolution.
    a. true
    b. false

7. *Mapp v. Ohio* and *Miranda v. Arizona* were landmark Warren Court decisions.
    a. true
    b. false

8. The jurisdiction of the U.S. Supreme Courts is almost completely mandatory.
    a. true
    b. false

9. Defendants convicted of violent offenses and sentenced to lengthy prison terms are more likely to win on appeal than those convicted of less serious offenses.
    a. true
    b. false

10. A *collateral attack* on a criminal conviction is a civil proceeding.
    a. true
    b. false

11. Under the new judicial federalism, state Supreme Courts are important policymakers in controversial areas.
    a. true
    b. false

12. Most of the U.S. Supreme Court's opinions are civil case decisions.
    a. true
    b. false

13. One of the most famous Warren Court decisions was *Brown v. Board of Education*.
    a. true
    b. false

14. Since 1980, the U.S. Supreme Court has shown steadily increasing support for the rights of criminal defendants.
    a. true
    b. false

15. Trial court filings are increasing faster than appellate filings.
    a. true
    b. false

Fill in the Blank

1. The famous _____ Court decision that ordered desegregation of public schools was *Brown v. Board of Education*.

2. In most states, intermediate appellate courts jurisdiction is _____.

3. An opinion in a case in which all of the appellate court judges participated is called an _____ *banc* decision.

4. The party who initiates or files an appeal is called the appellee or _____.

5. The ban on double jeopardy in found in the _____ Amendment.

6. After exhausting all appeals, convicts can again obtain review of their conviction by use of the writ of *habeas* _____.

7. A court announces and explains its decision in a written _____.

8. Most appellate decisions are rendered by _____ judge panels.

9. One of the functions of appellate court is _____ formulation or creation.

10. Most of the jurisdiction of the U.S. Supreme Court is _____.

11. Judges who disagree with the majority opinion author _____ opinions.

12. If a case is _____ by the appellate court, this means that the appellate court agreed with the lower court.

13. The current Chief Justice of the U.S. Supreme Court is John _____.

14. The newest Justice of the U.S. Supreme Court is Samuel _____.

15 Activism by state Supreme Court based on state constitutions is termed the new judicial _____.

Essay

1. List the current Justices on the U.S. Supreme Court. Identify the liberals, conservatives and swing vote.

2. Compare and contrast the Warren, Burger and Rehnquist Courts. Be sure to provide examples.

3. What are the two main functions or purposes of the appeal process? Provide an example of each.

4. Compare and contrast panel and *en banc* decisions. In general, what types of cases will be handled by each type of decision? Generally, what types of courts tend to use each type of decision? Be sure to provide examples.

5. Briefly discuss five important Warren Court decisions. Explain why each was important.

CHAPTER 17 ANSWER KEYS

Multiple Choice

1—a	2—d	3—d	4—b	5—c
6—a	7—c	8—b	9—c	10—b
11—a	12—b	13—c	14—c	15—c
16—c	17—b	18—a	19—c	20—a

True-False

1—F	2—F	3—T	4—T	5—F
6—T	7—F	8—F	9—F	10—T
11—T	12—T	13—T	14—F	15—F

Fill in the blank

1—Warren	2—mandatory	3—*en*	4.—petitioner
5—Fifth	6—*corpus*	7—opinion	8—three
9—policy	10—discretionary	11—dissenting	12—affirmed
13—Roberts	14—Alito	15—federalism	

Chapter 18
THE LOWER COURTS

LEARNING OBJECTIVES

After reading this chapter, student should understand the

- scope of felony, nonfelony, and civil cases in the lower courts.
- nature and extent of problems in the lower court.
- function and extent of rural justice.
- history and future of justice of the peace courts.
- role of municipal courts and the assembly line model of justice.
- sentencing process in the lower courts.
- relationship between courts and community collaboration.

CHAPTER OUTLINE

I.   **Scope of the Lower Courts**
    A.   Approximately 17,943 courts (60% of courts)
    B.   Sixty-four million case filings (two-thirds of all state court filings)
    C.   Felony Criminal Cases
    D.   Nonfelony Criminal Cases
        1.   Misdemeanor trials
        2.   Traffic offenses
        3.   Ordinance violations
    E.   Civil Cases
        1.   Small claims (civil)

II. **Problems of the Lower Courts**
    A.   Inadequate Financing
    B.   Inadequate Facilities
    C.   Lax Court Procedures
    D.   Unbalanced Caseloads

III. **Rural Justice**
    A.   Nearly 80 percent of courts of general jurisdiction are in rural areas
    B.   Lower Caseloads
    C.   Lack of Resources
    D.   Familiarity
        1.   Informal mechanisms of social control
    E.   Assessing Rural Justice
        1.   Local customs and interests may prevail over due process
        2.   May be bias against outsiders, minorities, etc.

IV. **Justice of the Peace Courts**
    A.   History in England and the U.S.
    B.   Most JPs are part-time non-lawyer locals

C. Abolition of the JP System
    1. Court reformers call for abolition of JP Court
    2. Appeals are by a new trial (trial *de novo*) in a higher court
D. Upgrading the Quality of the Personnel
    1. Only 5 percent of JPs were college graduates

V. Municipal Courts

A. Urban counterparts of the JP courts
B. Assembly Line
    1. Mass processing of cases without individual case consideration
    2. Few trials are held
C. The Courtroom Work Group
D. Sentencing
    1. Sentencing process involves routinization and individualization
    2. Nature of crime and defendant's prior record are prime considerations in sentencing
E. Is the Process the Punishment?
    1. Some critics suggest that the pretrial process is so costly and inefficient that the process is the punishment

VI. Court-Community Collaboration

A. Alternative Dispute Resolution (ADR) programs attempt to find informal solutions to minor civil and criminal problems in the community
B. Community Dispute Settlement Centers
    1. Mediation programs
    2. Often sponsored by private organizations
C. Community Courts
    1. Community courts attempt to utilize community resources to solve problems
    2. Removes minor cases from government criminal courts

VII. Conclusion

KEY TERMS

alternative dispute resolution **(ADR)** - Less adversarial means of settling disputes that may or may not involve a court. (414)

inferior court **(lower court)** - Term for a trial court of limited jurisdiction; also may refer to any court lower in the judicial hierarchy. (402)

justice of the peace **(JP)** - A low-level judge, sometimes without legal training, typically found in rural areas of some states, empowered to try petty civil and criminal cases and to conduct the preliminary stages of felony cases. (407)

misdemeanor - Lesser of the two basic types of crime, usually punishable by no more than one year in jail. (403)

municipal court - A trial court of limited jurisdiction created by a local unit of government. (408)

ordinance - A law enacted by a local government body for the regulation of some activity within the community. (403)

small claims court - A lower-level court whose jurisdiction is limited to a specific dollar amount—for example, damages not exceeding $1,500. (403)

traffic offenses - A group of offenses, including infractions and minor misdemeanors, relating to the operation of self-propelled motor vehicles. (403)

trial court of limited jurisdiction - A lower-level state court, such as a justice of the peace court, whose jurisdiction is limited to minor civil disputes or misdemeanors. (402)

CHAPTER SUMMARY

The lowest trial courts in the system, often referred to as trial courts of limited jurisdiction (TCLJ) are the most numerous courts and process about two-thirds of all cases. They sometimes handle the preliminary steps in felony cases. They have jurisdiction over misdemeanor offenses, traffic offenses, and ordinance violations. They also handle small civil suits. In some jurisdictions, these courts are also small claims courts. Small claims courts utilize expedited, informal procedures and a lawyer is not necessary.

In general, TCLJs utilize assembly line justice, especially in criminal cases. In both civil and criminal cases, people do not have attorneys. These courts tend to suffer from inadequacies in funding and facilities. Some have heavy caseloads and others have light caseloads, but there is no mechanism to shift cases to less-burdened courts.

The typical rural TCLJ is the Justice of the Peace Court. This court has a long history in both England and the U.S. The judges tend to be part-time non-lawyers. Critics question whether outsiders and minorities can get a fair hearing in such local courts. Appeal from these courts are by a new trial (trial *de novo*) in a higher court. However, this type of appeal does not allow for education by error correction of TCLJ judges. Reformers have called for the abolition of these courts but have generally not been successful. Many jurisdictions now provide training for these judges.

In cities, the typical TCLJ is the Municipal Court. These courts typically have high caseloads and assembly-line justice. Courtroom workgroups put a premium on moving the cases. As in higher criminal courts, the nature of the offense and the defendant's prior record are the primary factors in plea bargaining and sentencing. Researcher Malcolm Feeley argued that the process in TCLJ's is the primary criminal punishment. The cost, delay, night in jail, etc., are more disruptive than the actual sentence. Other researchers disagree with Feeley.

In many states are attempting to work more closely with the local community to find non-judicial solutions to disputes. There are a number of types of Alternative Dispute Resolution (ADR) programs that try to provide less adversarial means of settling disputes. Some communities have set up community dispute settlement centers or community courts to try to use mediation to solve problems.

PRACTICE TEST BANK

Multiple Choice

1. Appeals from a lower court that takes the form of a totally new trial is called a _____.
    a. trial *de novo*
    b. mandamus
    c. certiorari
    d. bench trial

2. In _____ (1976), the U.S. Supreme Court found no due process or equal protection violations in having non-lawyer judges in lower courts.
    a. *Tenny v. Breedlove*
    b. *Argersinger v. Hamlin*
    c. *Baldwin v. N.Y.*
    d. *North v. Russell*

3. According to researcher Malcolm _____, in lower courts the process is the punishment.
    a. O'Reilly
    b. Johnson
    c. Feeley
    d. Consolo

4. _____ attempts to find solutions to disputes through compromise and bargaining.
    a. Arbitration
    b. Mediation
    c. Conscription
    d. Conflagration

5. Which of the following is not a trial court of limited jurisdiction?
    a. court of common pleas
    b. small claims court
    c. justice of the peace court
    d. municipal court

6. The most frequent criminal sanction in lower courts is _____.
    a. a fine
    b. jail time
    c. excoriation
    d. probation

7. Trial courts of limited jurisdiction constitute about _____ percent of all courts.
    a. 50
    b. 60
    c. 70
    d. 80

8. Trial courts of limited jurisdiction try _____ civil cases.
    a. class action
    b. small claims
    c. anti-trust
    d. diversity jurisdiction

9. There are nearly _____ million annual case filings in trial courts of limited jurisdiction.
    a. 64
    b. 71
    c. 81
    d. 91

10. State lower court case filings are about _____ of all annual filings.
    a. one-fourth
    b. one-half
    c. one-third
    d. two-thirds

11. Which of the following would not be something that a lower court would likely do in a felony case?
    a. sentencing
    b. initial appearance
    c. issuing warrants
    d. preliminary hearing

12. Which of the following is not typical of lower court proceedings?
    a. informal
    b. presence of counsel for both parties
    c. nonjudicial atmosphere
    d. rapid processing

13. Defendants have a Sixth Amendment right to a jury trial only if the offense is punishable by incarceration of more than _____ months.
    a. two
    b. four
    c. six
    d. twelve

14. The U.S. Supreme Court held in *Argersinger v. Hamlin* (1972) that under the Sixth Amendment right to an attorney _____.
    a. the right exists if the possible sentence includes incarceration
    b. the right applies only in federal courts
    c. all misdemeanor defendants are entitled to an attorney
    d. no defendant denied an attorney can be incarcerated

15. Which of the following is not considered characteristic of lower courts?
    a. inadequate facilities
    b. assembly line justice
    c. lack of resources
    d. jury trials

16. As compared to urban lower courts, rural lower courts rely more on _____.
    a. local familiarity and customs
    b. adversarial proceedings
    c. impartial juries
    d. assembly line justice

17. Courtroom workgroups in municipal courts _____.
    a. resist assembly-line justice
    b. maintain adversarial relationships
    c. facilitate rapid movement of cases
    d. are less familiar with each other than in higher-level courts

18. Which of the following is not a common recommendation of court reformers?
    a. abolish non-lawyer judges
    b. abolish JP courts
    c. create a 3-tier court system
    d. increase the use of trial *de novo*

19. ADR stands for _____.
    a. Accelerated Disposition Rehabilitation
    b. Alternative Dispute Resolution
    c. Associated Dispute Rectification
    d. Active Differential Rectification

20. Which of the following is not considered a major problem of lower courts?
    a. insufficient financing
    b. utilization of technicalities and loopholes
    c. numerous difficult defense attorneys
    d. low qualifications of judges

True-False

1. In *North v. Russell*, the U.S. Supreme Court held that having non-lawyer judges violated due process.
    a. true
    b. false

2.   Typically, lower courts are funded on a statewide basis.
     a.   true
     b.   false

3.   Urban lower courts generally have heavier caseloads than rural lower courts.
     a.   true
     b.   false

4.   The American Justice of the Peace Court has its origins in France.
     a.   true
     b.   false

5.   Lower courts typically try landlord-tenant dispute cases.
     a.   true
     b.   false

6.   Small claims courts generally offer jury trials to settle cases.
     a.   true
     b.   false

7.   Lower trial courts are usually not considered courts of record.
     a.   true
     b.   false

8.   Under the Sixth Amendment, anyone charged with a misdemeanor punishable by incarceration of more than six months has a right to an attorney.
     a.   true
     b.   false

9.   In municipal courts, defendants usually make only one appearance.
     a.   true
     b.   false

10. Most trials in lower courts are jury trials.
     a.   true
     b.   false

11. In lower courts, most convicted misdemeanor defendants are sentenced to jail.
     a.   true
     b.   false

12. Lower courts are sometimes called trial courts of general jurisdiction.
     a.   true
     b.   false

13. Reformers have been very successful in abolishing lower courts.
    a. true
    b. false

14. Most lower court defendants are represented by an attorney.
    a. true
    b. false

15. The Sixth Amendment gives everyone charged with an offense that is potentially punishable by incarceration a right to a jury trial.
    a. true
    b. false

Fill in the Blank

1. Appeals from many lower court decisions take the form of a trial _____ *novo*.

2. Alternative dispute _____ is an alternative to formal court proceedings.

3. According to Malcolm Feeley, the process is the _____ in lower courts.

4. Lower courts usually try cases involving, misdemeanors, ____violations, and traffic offenses.

5. Misdemeanors are typically punishable by a maximum of less than one _____ in jail.

6. County or city regulations or laws are referred to as _____.

7. Small _____ courts are lower courts providing expedited procedures for resolution of minor civil disputes.

8. Most trial courts of limited jurisdiction are not courts of _____.

9 The J.P. court traces its origins to fourteenth century _____.

10. A current trend is to increase court-_____ cooperation.

11. The most frequent form of punishment in lower courts is a _____.

12. Most trial courts of limited jurisdiction are funded by _____ government(s).

13. In North v. Russell the U.S. Supreme Court found no constitutional violations in lower courts having _____ judges.

14. Lower courts constitute around _____ percent of all judicial bodies.

15. In the U.S., there are approximately _____ thousand lower courts.

Essay

1.   Compare and contrast lower courts in rural and urban areas.

2.   Under what circumstances does a criminal defendant have a right to an attorney and a jury trial under the Sixth Amendment? What is the impact of these rules on lower courts?

3.   Discuss three problems common to both rural and urban lower courts.

4.   Discuss two types of programs courts are using to increase community involvement in dispute resolution. Be sure to provide examples.

5.   What are some of the various types of civil and criminal cases tried in lower courts? Be sure to provide examples.

CHAPTER 18 ANSWER KEYS

Multiple Choice

1—a	2—d	3—c	4—b	5—a
6—a	7—b	8—b	9—a	10—d
11—a	12—b	13—c	14—d	15—d
16—a	17—c	18—d	19—b	20—c

True-False

1—F	2—F	3—T	4—F	5—T
6—F	7—T	8—F	9—T	10—F
11—F	12—F	13—F	14—F	15—F

Fill in the blank

1—*de*	2—resolution	3—punishment	4.—ordinance
5—year	6—ordinances	7—claims	8—record
9—England	10—community	11—fines	12—local
13—nonlawyer	14—sixty	15—eighteen	

Chapter 19
JUVENILE COURTS

LEARNING OBJECTIVES

After reading this chapter, students should understand the

- historical evolution of the juvenile justice system.
- variances between adult and juvenile courts.
- organization and jurisdiction of juvenile courts.
- nature and extent of due process in juvenile courts.
- impact of the courtroom work group on juvenile proceedings.
- various steps of the juvenile court process.
- future and continued evolution of juvenile courts.

CHAPTER OUTLINE

I. **Juvenile Courts 100 Years Ago**
    A.   Industrialization, Cities, and Crime
        1.   Impact of immigration and poverty
    B.   The Child Savers and the Progressive Movement
        1.   Part of Progressive Movement (1890-1929)
        2.   Elite and middle-class reformers who wanted to help children
    C.   *Parens Patriae*
        1.   Justifies intervening to assist children

II. **How the Juvenile Courts Differ from Adult Courts**
    A.   Emphasis on Helping the Child
    B.   Informal Proceedings
    C.   Proceedings Based on Civil Law
    D.   Secret Proceedings
    E.   Absence of Jury Trials

III. **The Organization of Juvenile Courts**
    A.   Juvenile Court as a Separate Court
    B.   Juvenile Court as part of a Family Court
    C.   Juvenile Court as a Unit of Trial Court
    D.   Law in Action: The Impact of Structure
        1.   Reformers advocate making it part of a family court system
        2.   Structure probably has less impact than social environment

III. **Juvenile Court Jurisdiction: Age**
    A.   No Consensus on Age of Juveniles
    B.   Transfer to Adult Court
        1.   Most charges with violent crime likely to be transferred
        2.   Disproportionate number of minority males are transferred

IV. Juvenile Court Jurisdiction: Subject Matter
A. Juvenile Delinquency
1. Delinquency offenses are offenses that would also be crimes for adults
B. Status Offenses
1. Status offenses are offenses that can only be committed by juveniles
C. Child-Victim
1. Some courts also deal with child neglect and dependency cases
D. Law in Action: One-Pot Jurisdiction
1. Serious crimes, status offenders, and deprived children in one pot

V. Due Process in Juvenile Courts
A. Key Court Decisions
1. *In re Gault* (1967), due process applies to juvenile courts
2. Recent conservative Supreme Courts have been less willing to expand the rights of juveniles
B. Important Congressional Acts
1. Federal Juvenile Justice and Delinquency Prevention Act of 1974 mandated deinstitutionalization of status offenders
2. Juvenile court is becoming more open to public scrutiny

VI. Courtroom Work Group
A. Prior record, severity of offense and capabilities of parent important factors
B. Significant reliance on psychologists, social workers, etc.
C. Judges
1. Judges have wider discretion than in criminal court
D. Hearing Officers
1. Some jurisdictions use hearing officers rather than judges
E. Prosecutors
1. Juvenile court is not a high-status assignment
F. Defense Attorneys
1. Secondary actors and frequently not utilized
G. Probation Officers
1. Probation officers have roles similar to those in criminal court
a. Prepare background reports
b. Supervise juveniles on probation

VII. Steps of the Juvenile Court Process
A. Delinquency (Crime)
B. Summons (Arrest)
C. Intake (Initial Hearing)
D. Detention Hearing
E. Petition
F. Conference
G. Evidence: Gathering and Suppressing
H. Plea Bargaining
I. Adjudicatory Hearing

J.   Disposition
K.   Appeal

VIII. Juvenile Courts: The Next 100 Years
    A.   Crime Control Model: More Adult Penalties
        1.   Increase transfers to adult court
        2.   Some advocate abolition of juvenile court
    B.   Due Process Model: More Youth Crime Prevention
        1.   Addressing social problems for prevention
        2.   Concern for mistreatment of housing youth with adults

IX.   Conclusion

KEY TERMS

adjudicated - Judicial determination (judgment) that a youth is a delinquent or status offender. (440)

adjudicatory hearing - Court hearing to determine whether a youth is guilty or not guilty. (440)

child-victim - Juvenile court case involving a child who has been neglected and/or abused by the parents. (429)

conference - Juvenile court proceeding roughly equivalent to a preliminary hearing, in which the suspect is informed of his or her rights and a disposition decision may be reached. (438)

delinquency - An act committed by a juvenile that would require an adult to be prosecuted in a criminal court. Because the act is committed by a juvenile, it falls within the jurisdiction of the juvenile court. Delinquent acts include crimes against persons or property, drug offenses, and crimes against public order. (438)

detention - Holding a youth in custody before case disposition. (438)

dismissal - Cases terminated (including those warned, counseled, and released) with no further disposition anticipated. (440)

disposition - A court decision on what will happen to a youth who has not been found innocent. (440)

initial hearing - In juvenile court, an often informal hearing during which an intake decision is made. (438)

intake decision - The decision made by a juvenile court that results in the case being handled either informally at the intake level or more formally by petition and scheduled for an adjudicatory or transfer hearing. (438)

juvenile - Youth at or below the upper age of juvenile court jurisdiction. (425)

juvenile court - Any court that has jurisdiction over matters involving juveniles. (423)

lower age of jurisdiction - Minimum age at which a youth may be transferred to adult court. (425)

nonpetitioned case - A case handled informally by duly authorized court personnel. (438)

other dispositions - Miscellaneous dispositions, including fines, restitution, community service, and referrals outside the court for services, with minimal or no further court involvement anticipated. (441)

parens patriae - The state as parent; the state as guardian and protector of all citizens (such as juveniles) who are unable to protect themselves. (423)

petition - A document filed in juvenile court alleging that a juvenile is a delinquent or a status offender and asking that the court assume jurisdiction over the juvenile or that an alleged delinquent be transferred to criminal court for prosecution as an adult. (438)

placement - Cases in which youths are placed in a residential facility or otherwise removed from their homes and placed elsewhere. (440)

probation - Punishment for a crime that allows the offender to remain in the community without incarceration but subject to certain conditions (440)

probation officer - Employee of probation agency, responsible for supervision of convicted offenders who have been released to the community under certain conditions of good behavior. (434)

referral - A request by a law enforcement agency, governmental agency, parent, or individual that a juvenile court take jurisdiction of a youth. A referral initiates court processing. (437)

status offense - Behavior that is considered an offense only when committed by a juvenile—for example, running away from home. (429)

summons - A legal document ordering an individual to appear in court at a certain time on a certain date. (437)

transfer to criminal court - A case is moved to a criminal court because of a waiver or transfer (426)

upper age of jurisdiction - The oldest age at which a juvenile court has original jurisdiction over an individual for behavior that violates the law. (425)

CHAPTER SUMMARY

Juvenile courts began in the late twentieth century. The major economic and social changes of the late nineteenth century prompted a rethinking of the role of youth. The result was the creation of specialized courts to deal with what were thought to be distinctly youth-oriented problems.

Beginning around 1890, members of the Progressive Movement advocated a variety of political, economic, and social reforms. They were genuinely concerned about the economic disparities, social disorders, and excesses of industrialization, particularly as they affected children. Among their concerns was the plight of poor, urban youth. One part of the Progressive Movement was termed the "Child Savers." This group of elite and middle-class reformers pushed for creation of special courts to help, rather than punish, juveniles.

By the end of the 1800s, the perception of children as miniature adults was fading. Children were seen as persons with less than fully developed moral and cognitive capacities. This shift in thinking was reflected in the legal doctrine of *parens patriae* (state as parent). No longer were parents considered to have sole and exclusive legal responsibility over their children. If the parents failed in their responsibility to raise a child properly, the state could intervene to protect the child's welfare. In extreme circumstances parental rights over their children could be terminated altogether.

The unique legal dimensions of juvenile court are reflected in the legal terms employed. Adults are arrested, tried, and sentenced to prison, whereas: juveniles are summoned, have a hearing, and are committed to residential placement. Juvenile courts differ from adult courts in five important ways: they emphasize helping the child, they are informal, they are based on civil law, they are secret, and they rarely involve jury trials.

Criminal prosecutions are formal and adversarial in nature. By contrast, juvenile court proceedings emphasize informality. Although key elements of due process have been integrated into juvenile court since the 1960s, juvenile proceedings nonetheless retain much of their informal nature. Juvenile court proceedings are based primarily on the civil law. This is why the legal terminology used in criminal and juvenile courts differs so greatly. The terms "summons" and "commitment," for example, are borrowed directly from civil practice.

Today, all states have juvenile courts, but their organizational structure varies greatly. Only a few states have created juvenile courts that are completely separate from other judicial bodies. Juvenile courts are organized in one of three ways: a separate court, part of family court, or a unit of a trial court.

Juvenile court jurisdiction is based on the age of the person and the acts they committed. For many states, once a person reaches age eighteen, they must go to criminal court. In terms of the acts, delinquency refers to crimes. Status offenses are offenses that can only be committed by juveniles. Many judges of family courts also hear dependency, neglect and abuse cases. In all states, juveniles who commit serious crimes can be transferred or waived to criminal court.

223

The steps in a typical juvenile case are as follows: (1) Delinquency (Crime), (2) Summons (Arrest), (3) Intake (Initial Hearing), (4) Detention Hearing, (5) Petition, (6) Conference, (7) Evidence gathering and suppressing, (8) Plea Bargaining, (9) Adjudicatory Hearing, (10) Disposition (sentencing), and (11) Appeal.

There is a courtroom work group in juvenile court just as in criminal court. Judges tend to have more discretion than in adult court, but the prosecutor is still, overall, the most powerful player. Defense attorneys play a secondary role or are not provided or utilized by juveniles. The lack of legal representation (or lack of quality and aggressive representation) is of concern to many. Plea bargaining is common in both criminal and juvenile court. Procedures are less formal in juvenile court and probation officers and experts (e.g., social workers) play a larger role in juvenile court.

In terms of sentencing or disposition, most juveniles get some form of formal or informal probation. Most communities have a variety of programs for juveniles. A few are placed in institutions.

The future of juvenile court is hard to predict. The debate is generally between the conservatives who advocate a crime control model stressing punishment, and liberals who advocate prevention and treatment.

PRACTICE TEST BANK

1.   Status offenses involve acts that _____.
        a.   violate status laws
        b.   are violations of the criminal law
        c.   can be committed by adults only
        d.   can be committed by juveniles only

2.   In addition to cases involving misconduct by children, juvenile courts also hear cases of:
        a.   child abuse and neglect.
        b.   crimes by corporations against juveniles.
        c.   foreign adoptions.
        d.   international rights of children.

3.   In the *Gault* decision, the U.S. Supreme Court held that juveniles _____.
        a.   can be subjected to preventive detention
        b.   have no right to grand jury review
        c.   are entitled to due process in juvenile court
        d.   are protected by the Fourth Amendment

4.   The federal Juvenile Justice and Delinquency Prevention Act of 1974 mandated the
        _____ of status offenders.
        a.   decreased use of counseling
        b.   increased use of bailing
        c.   execution
        d.   deinstitutionalization

5.   Over time, juvenile courts cases have moved from being primarily ____ cases to
        becoming more like criminal courts cases.
        a.   equity
        b.   chancery
        c.   ecclesiastical
        d.   civil

6.   The first juvenile court was created in ____ in 1899.
        a.   New York
        b.   Illinois
        c.   California
        d.   Texas

7.   In the _____ case, the U.S. Supreme Court held that delinquency must be proven
        beyond a reasonable doubt.
        a.   Winship
        b.   McKeiver
        c.   Gault
        d.   Schall

8. The U.S. Supreme Court first intervened in juvenile court proceedings in 1966 in the case of _____ v. U.S.
   a. *Channing*
   b. *Kent*
   c. *Cozort*
   d. *Miller*

9. _____ officers commonly prepare background reports on juveniles and supervise them.
   a. Hearing
   b. Court
   c. Parole
   d. Probation

10. A _____ is a legal document ordering someone to appear in court.
    a. *capias*
    b. information
    c. summons
    d. *certiorari*

11. The most frequent source of referral to juvenile court is from _____.
    a. law enforcement
    b. schools
    c. social welfare agencies
    d. informants

12. Roughly _____ percent of juveniles are detained prior to their adjudication hearing.
    a. 10
    b. 20
    c. 30
    d. 40

13. On any given day in the U.S., approximately _____ thousand juveniles are being held in public and private detention facilities.
    a. 50
    b. 100
    c. 150
    d. 200

14. Around _____ million persons under age eighteen are arrested each year in the U.S.
    a. 1.5
    b. 2.2
    c. 3.5
    d. 4.5

15. For both petitioned and nonpetitioned cases, the most frequent outcome for juveniles is
    _____.
    a. dismissal
    b. probation
    c. placement
    d. incarceration

16. The most frequently applied correctional sanction in juvenile court is _____.
    a. probation
    b. placement
    c. fine
    d. incarceration

17. Many states give juveniles a constitutional right to _____, but the Supreme Court has
    been reluctant to make it a Constitutional requirement.
    a. bail
    b. grand jury review
    c. jury trial
    d. appeal

18. The doctrine of _____ allows the government to intervene in the lives of children.
    a. *non compos mentos*
    b. *quid pro quo*
    c. *parens patriae*
    d. *nulla bona*

19. Juvenile courts were one of the reforms during the _____ era.
    a. Trust-buster
    b. Progressive
    c. Prohibition
    d. Manifest Destiny

20. When compared to adult criminal courts, which of the following is not characteristic of
    juvenile courts?
    a. informality
    b. civil law terminology
    c. secret proceedings
    d. jury trials

True-False

1. The original theory of the juvenile court was that it was to punish children.
    a. true
    b. false

2.   In some jurisdictions, juvenile courts are part of Family Courts.
     a.   true
     b.   false

3.   Juvenile courts are commonly part of an appellate court in most states.
     a.   true
     b.   false

4.   Most states consider persons to be juveniles until they reach age sixteen.
     a.   true
     b.   false

5.   Only about one percent of juvenile cases are transferred or waived to criminal court.
     a.   true
     b.   false

6.   In some states, there is no minimum age below which a child cannot be transferred to adult court.
     a.   true
     b.   false

7.   The Rehnquist Court has greatly expanded the rights of juveniles in juvenile court.
     a.   true
     b.   false

8.   There is no federal legislation dealing with how states should treat juvenile offenders.
     a.   true
     b.   false

9.   Over time, juvenile court procedures have become more similar to adult criminal court procedures.
     a.   true
     b.   false

10. Juveniles are not entitled to due process in juvenile court.
     a.   true
     b.   false

11. Juveniles have a Sixth Amendment right to a jury trial in juvenile court in 48 of the 50 states.
     a.   true
     b.   false

12. Juvenile court judges generally have greater discretion in their work than adult criminal court judges.
     a.   true
     b.   false

13. In juvenile court, the defense attorney is the most powerful member of the courtroom work group.
    a. true
    b. false

14. Juvenile crime rates have been increasing dramatically since 1995.
    a. true
    b. false

15. Juvenile court assignments are commonly high status positions for judges, prosecutors and defense attorneys.
    a. true
    b. false

Fill in the Blank

1. In addition to the type of act, _____ is another major determinant of juvenile court jurisdiction.

2. Most states consider children to be juveniles until they reach age _____.

3. If a juvenile case is adjudicated, this means the case went to _____.

4. In juvenile court, the conference is roughly equivalent to the _____ hearing in adult criminal cases.

5. In juvenile court, the sentencing stage is referred to as the _____.

6. The _____ decision commonly determines whether a case will be handled formally or informally.

7. A nonpetitioned case is one that will most likely be handled _____.

8. Only _____ can commit status offenses.

9. A juvenile court disposition where the juvenile is removed from the home is called a _____.

10. The _____ is equivalent to an indictment or information in an adult criminal case.

11. *Parens patriae* is the legal theory that the state has the power to act in place of the _____.

12. Transfer to criminal court is sometimes referred to as waiver or _____.

13. _____ involves confinement of the juvenile pending the adjudication hearing.

14.   In the _____ case, the U.S. Supreme Court held that juvenile courts must provide due process.

15.   The most frequently used corrective sanction in juvenile court is _____.

Essays

1. Discuss how the juvenile justice system evolved compared to the adult justice system.

2. Describe how the juvenile court process differs from the adult court process. Do you agree with the legal principle of *parens patriae*? Why or why not?

3. Discuss why some advocates contend the juvenile courts system should be abolished. What would be the benefits and disadvantages of eliminating the juvenile court system?

4. Describe how the courtroom work group impacts the nature of juvenile justice. How is the impact similar and how is it different than the influence the group has on the adult system of justice?

5. Discuss how the crime control and due process models of justice will likely impact the nature of juvenile justice in the future.

CHAPTER 19 ANSWER KEYS

Multiple Choice

1—d	2—a	3—c	4—d	5—d
6—b	7—a	8—b	9—d	10—c
11—a	12—b	13—b	14—b	15—a
16—a	17—d	18—c	19—b	20—d

True-False

1—F	2—T	3—F	4—F	5—T
6—T	7—F	8—F	9—T	10—F
11—F	12—T	13—F	14—F	15—F

Fill in the blank

1—age	2—18	3—trial	4—preliminary
5—disposition	6—intake	7—informally	8—juveniles
9—placement	10—petition	11—parents	12—certification
13—Detention	14—Gault	15—probation	